HOCKEY SUPERSTARS

HOCKEY SUPERSTARS

JOSEPH ROMAIN and JAMES DUPLACEY

SMITHMARK
PUBLISHERS INC.

Page 1: *Perhaps the greatest defenseman of all time, Bobby Orr set high-water marks in virtually every category available during his career with the Boston Bruins.*

Page 2: *Mario Lemieux leads his team to victory against the Chicago Black Hawks in the fourth and final game of the 1992 Stanley Cup finals.*

Page 3: *The New York Islanders' stellar Mike Bossy reached the 100-point plateau seven times, establishing himself as one of the NHL's greatest right wingers.*

Left: *Three future Hall of Famers, (left to right) Bernie Geoffrion, Jean Beliveau and Maurice Richard, made the Montreal Canadiens a force to be reckoned with during the fifties.*

This edition published in 1994
by SMITHMARK Publishers Inc.,
16 East 32nd Street,
New York, New York 10016.

SMITHMARK books are available for bulk purchase for sales promotion and premium use. For details write or telephone the Manager of Special Sales, SMITHMARK Publishers Inc., 16 East 32nd Street, New York, NY 10016. (212) 532-6600

Produced by Brompton Books Corp.
15 Sherwood Place
Greenwich, CT 06830

ISBN 0-8317-4508-8

Printed in China

10 9 8 7 6 5 4 3 2 1

Picture Credits

Bruce Bennett Studios: Bruce Bennett 2, 3, 7(bottom right), 17, 19(both), 29, 32, 33(bottom), 34, 35, 36-37, 44-45, 51, 61, 65(both), 77(top), 78, 89, 91, 94(top), 98, 99, 101; Melchior DiGiacomo 7(top right), 22, 23(both), 26(bottom right), 27, 75(top), 82, 84-85, 86, 87; Brian Winkler 50, 73; S. Levy 68-69, 77(bottom); Joe DiMaggio/Joanne Kalish 88; B. Miller 100, 109.
The Bettmann Archive, Inc.: 11, 104.
Hockey Hall of Fame and Museum, Toronto: 10, 13(top), 14-15, 20, 21, 24, 26(top left), 28, 30, 31, 33(top), 38, 39, 40, 41(bottom), 42, 43, 46, 47(bottom), 48, 49, 52-53, 62, 63, 66, 67, 70, 74, 75(bottom), 79, 80, 83, 90, 94(bottom), 95, 102, 103(top), 106, 107, 108, 110, 111.
UPI/Bettmann Newsphotos: 4, 6(top both), 7(bottom left), 8-9, 12, 13(bottom), 16, 18, 25, 41(top), 47(top), 54, 55, 56, 57, 58-59, 60, 64, 71(both), 72, 76, 81, 92, 93(both), 96, 97(both), 103(bottom), 105.

Acknowledgments

The authors and publisher would like to thank the following people who have helped in the preparation of this book: Barbara Thrasher, who edited it; Don Longabucco, who designed it; Sara Antonecchia, who did the picture research; and Florence Norton, who prepared the index.

CONTENTS

INTRODUCTION

To earn a place on a National Hockey League team a man has to be physically strong, highly skilled, disciplined and dedicated; to win a regular shift requires additional traits, including durability and innovation. To stand out in this elite pack a skater has to have something pretty special; he has the skills and makeup, but he also has to shine. The following pages tell the stories of the men who have risen above this cream of the winter crop, by shooting, stopping, and checking their way into the history books. These are the superstars of hockey; they have achieved their boyhood dreams and are the beacons of coming generations.

While it is true that every man we chose to represent the vanguard of hockey stardom belongs here, it is also true that there are others we could have just as easily included. Every generation has its crop of superstars, but there is just not room for all of them in a work of this size. This is not the Hockey Hall of Fame, but a rather more selective look at the hockey constellation. The goal of this book is to give the reader a sense of who these men are, and what they did to become household names across two countries.

The superstars we included will not all be immediately familiar to all the readers; they range in time from the turn of the century to the present day, and many of the early stars set records which have long been forgotten. When Howie Morenz was hockey's premier skater, the feats of Wayne Gretzky would have ranked with those of Paul Bunyan. But just as Bunyan had no chain saw, Morenz had no center red line and only 48 games in his longest season.

Some of our current superstars may in the end turn out to be shooting stars; history is full of men who make tremendous strides, stumble, and are never heard from again. But they are no less superstars for that: Superstar recognition is based on brilliance in the night sky and not always on the longevity of the glow. Charlie Conacher, one of the most colorful men of his time, had only five great seasons before drifting into relative obscurity, but from 1930 to 1935, he lit up rinks from New York to Chicago.

Today, superstar status means a ticket to the fat of the land. We reward our most brilliant athletes with riches beyond the dreams of mere mortals, but this too has a tradition. When Cyclone Taylor was shooting and scoring, he was paid like a prince, making considerably more money in his day than Ty Cobb, with whom he was often compared.

Hockey is entertainment, and these are the Clark Gables and Robert Redfords of the ice rinks. They are larger than life, overachievers in a world where output is everything, and idolized by young and old; from Howie Morenz to Pavel Bure, these are the superstars of hockey.

Opposite left: *The great Wayne Gretzky holds up the puck he used to score his record-breaking 1,851st point in 1989.*

Opposite right: *Hockey super-stars (left to right) Denis Potvin, Bryan Trottier and Mike Bossy hold aloft the Stanley Cup after the 1981 finals.*

Right: *The Boston Bruins' hockey phenomenon, Bobby Orr, was elected to the Hall of Fame in 1979.*

Below: *Perpetual All-Star center Phil Esposito led the NHL in scoring five times.*

Below right: *Larry Robinson twice won the James Norris Memorial Trophy as the NHL's best defenseman.*

Overleaf: *Bobby Hull (left) and Stan Mikita – superstar teammates.*

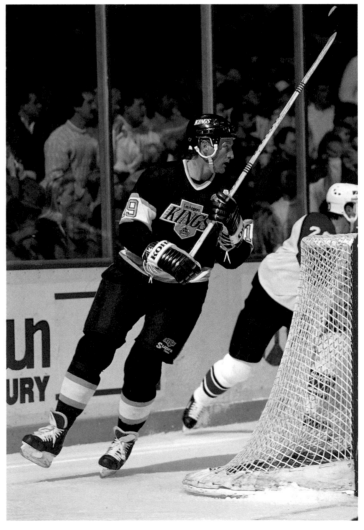

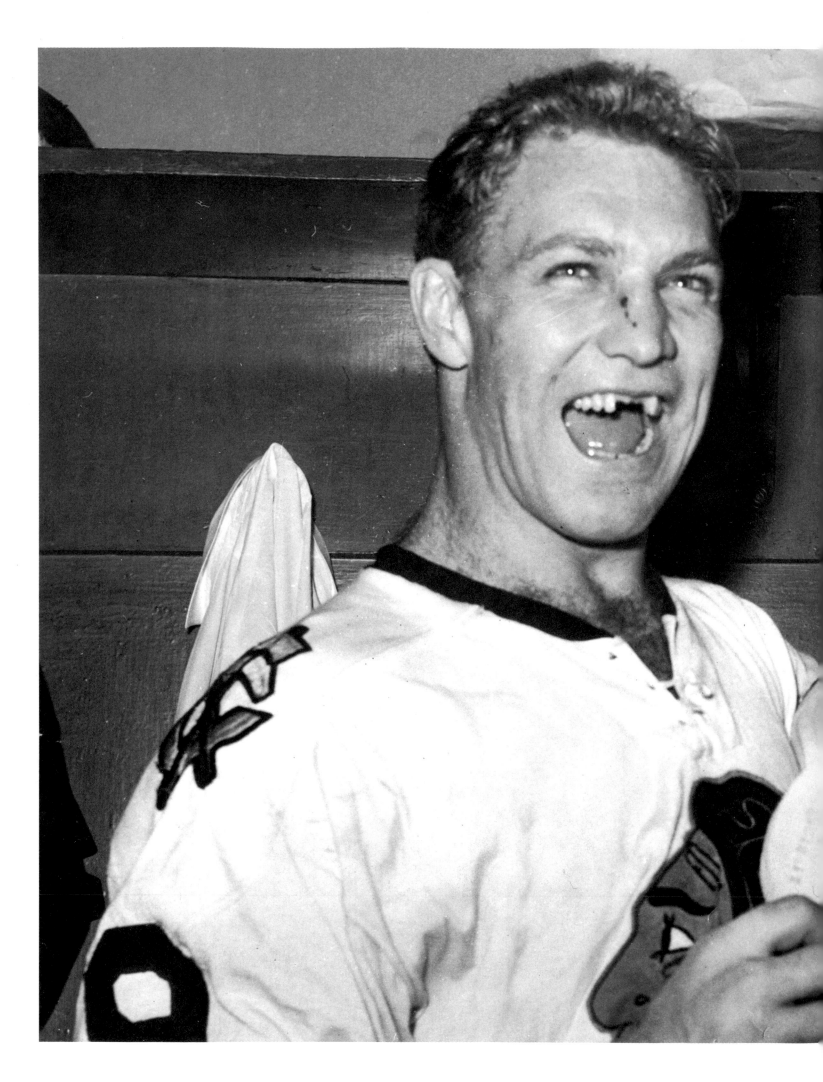

CYCLONE TAYLOR

Fred "Cyclone" Taylor was probably hockey's first true superstar. Playing as he did in a time when a hefty percentage of skaters were Hall of Fame bound, Taylor outshone all of his peers. It was not his powerful scoring ability that brought the fans out in droves to see him, although in his 180 career games he scored 194 goals, including 16 hat tricks; neither was it his complete domination of every game he played that made him one of the highest paid athletes of his day. Taylor's claim to fame was his unique ability to reverse his stride, and skate backwards!

Today, every youngster worthy of his skates can perform this trick with ease, but in Taylor's early career, the stunt was almost unheard of. Bill Galloway, one of the premier historians of the game, has it from Newsy Lalonde that Taylor learned the feat from an itinerant carnival skater who showed Fred Taylor how to file the back end of his blade "just so." The rest is history. When All-Star teams of the National Hockey Association were invited to tour the northeastern United States, the hockey impresarios insisted that without Taylor, the deal was off.

Taylor played his early pro games with the International Hockey League in upstate Michigan, but returned to Canada in 1908 to play with Ottawa and Renfrew of the National Hockey Association. He played his best 10 years on the West Coast, on the Pacific Coast Hockey Association's Vancouver team, where he spun his way into the Hockey Hall of Fame.

The city of Ottawa went out of its way to make Taylor

Left: *Cyclone Taylor was the most exciting player of his day. He was highly skilled, led great teams, and most of all, he was the only man who had mastered the art of skating backwards!*

Opposite: *Taylor played on organized teams in many leagues, but he made much of his money on exhibition tours throughout Canada and the United States. He was inducted in the Hall of Fame in 1945.*

happy and comfortable while shooting and scoring for their Eastern Canadian Hockey Association franchise. They arranged a good civil service job for him in the off-season, and they encouraged his public exhibitions around Canada and the United States. Taylor, however, was a pragmatist, and when the O'Brien family of Renfrew, Ontario, formed the National Hockey Association and the Renfrew Million-aires, Taylor took a long look at his career prospects. O'Brien rounded up the best hockey players in the country for the sole purpose of winning the cherished Stanley Cup. He brought Lester and Frank Patrick from the West Coast, paid them unheard-of salaries, and went after the biggest box office draw of the day: Cyclone Taylor. Taylor was no

fool; he took the money and moved down the road to Ren-frew, where the new team was expected to shatter all com-ers. The story goes that Taylor boasted that when his Millionaires met his old Ottawa squad, he would skate the length of the ice backwards and score with his back to the net. Taylor, in later life, claimed never to have achieved the feat, but there are still residents of the Ottawa Valley who claim that they were there to see it happen!

When the Patrick brothers moved back to the West Coast to form their own league, they took Cyclone Taylor with them. At 29 years of age he was still the premier player in the league, and he continued to please the roaring crowd with 10 more years of superstar caliber hockey.

GEORGES VEZINA

When a goaltender in the National Hockey League has a zenith season, they give him a trophy named after the most sensational goaltender of the early days of the game. That man was Georges Vezina, and his legacy is as formidable as the trophy is difficult to earn.

He was born in Chicoutimi, Quebec, in 1888, and broke in with the Montreal Canadiens in 1911, long before the National Hockey League was born. Hockey was a high-scoring game in those National Hockey Association days, but the man to beat was Georges Vezina. He was a standup goaltender, as was the hockey law in his day, and he was as cool a customer as ever protected the twine.

The Habs are reputed to have discovered Vezina the hard way. The team was on an exhibition tour when they visited the northern town of Chicoutimi, and met the local heroes for a fund-raising scrimmage. Though the Montrealers had some of the best men in the business stickhandling through the blur of hometown boys, they could not get the

better of this six-footer between the frozen pipes. The Montreal squad left Chicoutimi with a 2-0 black eye, but that eye would soon turn back upon the northern town when the team management went shopping for a goaltender. A handshake later, the Montreal Canadiens had one of the best puck-stoppers in history ready for the NHA season.

Vezina led the Habs to victory game after game, and in the 15 seasons he played, they were league champions five times, and Stanley Cup winners twice. When he arrived to train for the 1925-26 season it was clear that something was wrong. He perspired profusely in the cold of the arena, and he seemed to tire without explanation. Only Vezina knew that he was dying, and when the season opened against Pittsburgh, he played his last hockey.

Georges Vezina died later that season, of advanced tuberculosis. A member of the Hockey Hall of Fame, Georges Vezina will be remembered as one of the finest goaltenders ever to step between the pipes.

Left: *Georges Vezina spent virtually all of his adult life playing hockey. From the time that the Habs picked up this kid in Chicoutimi, Quebec, in 1911 until tuberculosis halted his play and claimed his life in 1926, he never missed a game.*

Opposite: *Vezina played goal in the days when a puckstopper was prohibited from dropping to the ice. Given this regulation, his career 3.45 goals against average is all the more remarkable.*

HOWIE MORENZ

The stories of Howie Morenz illustrate something important about superstars; he reminds us that they are as human as the rest of us.

As the story goes, Howie and his buddy were meandering home following a night of bending elbows and losing at the card table. Morenz, who had lost some money on the evening, flipped the 50-cent piece he'd been jingling in his pocket over his shoulder and into the empty street. His companion, knowing the value of 50 cents in the 1920s, laughed at him, and asked him what he was doing. Howie chuckled and mused; some kid would get lucky and pocket the four-bit piece, and Howie Morenz, the thoroughbred ice horse, knew a thing or two about luck.

The "Stratford Streak" was one of the very biggest names in the game. He was the league's Most Valuable Player in 1928, 1931 and 1932, led all scorers in 1928 and 1931, and was the proud member of three Stanley Cup winning sides. In a time when every hockey town had larger-than-life hockey superstars, Howie Morenz was the most well-known name in hockey. Often compared to Babe Ruth, Morenz differs from Ruth in his almost complete obliteration from the record book.

To put Howie Morenz's superstar status into perspective, consider the context in which he played. In 1931 Morenz won the Art Ross Trophy as the league's leader in points. He scored 28 goals and 23 assists in a year when the entire Montreal Canadien team scored fewer goals than Wayne Gretzky earned points 50 years later!

Howie Morenz's untimely injury on the ice and subsequent early death in 1937 is one of the great tragedies of the game. He was laid out at the Montreal Forum, where thousands jammed in to pay their respects. His grief-stricken family was the beneficiary of the proceeds from an All-Star Game played in his honor, and the legend of Howie Morenz, the "Mitchell Meteor," is still among the most remembered and revered in hockey lore.

Opposite: *The Mitchell Meteor, the Stratford Streak, the Mighty Mite – call him what you like, but Howie Morenz was the most exciting hockey player of his day. His dashes from end to end left the opposition bewildered and the fans on the edge of their seats during the 1920s and 1930s.*

Right: *The untimely death of Howie Morenz is one of the great tragedies of the game. In the midst of a great comeback with the Habs, Morenz's leg was irreparably broken, and after a long stint in the hospital, he died of complications unrelated to his injury.*

15

KING CLANCY

Left: *King Clancy is not best known as a whistle-blower, but it was one of the many roles he played in professional hockey after hanging up his blades in 1938. As a referee Clancy patrolled the ice during the 1940s, and is known as one of the fairest ice judges in the history of the game.*

Opposite: *A young King Clancy in his Ottawa Senators uniform. Clancy spent most of his first two years with Ottawa in an unheated dressing room, waiting for a bell which called him into the fray. Once on the ice, he earned his money, and then some: in 1930 he brought a cash-poor Ottawa squad $35,000 when they sold him to Conn Smythe's Maple Leafs for the highest sum ever spent on a puck-chaser.*

When Toronto Maple Leaf owner Conn Smythe approached his board of directors with a proposal to purchase the Ottawa Senators' key defenseman Michael Francis "King" Clancy for $35,000, he was met with wagging heads and guffaws all around. After all, in 1931, $35,000 was enough to purchase any three National League players, and Clancy was only half the size of any of them.

At 5'7", this 155-pound backliner might have been a joke, but sorry would be the forward who passed into Clancy's zone without proper respect. Though he lost plenty of fights, he left quite a few bruises around the league, and never avoided the confrontations that are the stock and trade of big league defensemen.

He was not a great skater, but his unique manner of running on the blades to gather speed made for great entertainment, and allowed King to cover the best gliders in the business. His opponents were Joliat, Morenz, Ebbie Goodfellow, Mush March, and the Cook brothers – all men who would look for this feisty little guy as they stickhandled into the Toronto zone. Though they saw him as a formidable adversary, nobody called this man his enemy.

King Clancy was proof that leprechauns exist; and that they can skate! Always ready with a prank, King kept the boys in stitches between games, and provided the light-hearted leadership that made the team a family affair. Clancy brought an unassailable Irish cheerfulness to the entire hockey community. He was at his peak during the Great Depression, but Clancy always gave fans, foes and friends something to smile about.

But King Clancy was not the court jester of the National Hockey League; he was a fine defenseman, and showed the kind of gritty determination that is required of the job. Though he may be the smallest defenseman ever to play big league hockey, he was selected to four All-Star teams, won three Stanley Cups as a player, and was inducted into the Hockey Hall of Fame for his on-ice skills.

EDDIE SHORE

Opposite: *The notice on the board says it all for defenseman Eddie Shore: Positively No Fast Skating Allowed. This four-time All-Star led the Bruins to their first Stanley Cup championship in 1928-29.*

Right: *Of Eddie Shore it's been written: "Nobody in the game's history has achieved that perfect blend of skill and violence which was the hallmark of the Bruins' Fighting Star."* Ed Fitzgerald (Sport Magazine, *February 1950)*

Eddie Shore is best remembered as one of the bad boys of hockey; but Shore did more than bash and grind his way through the 1920s and 1930s. In those days of star-studded lineups, Shore took the Hart Trophy as the National Hockey League's Most Valuable Player on four separate occasions, was a seven-time All-Star, and led the Bruins to their first two Stanley Cup championships.

He reached double figures in goals scored five times, an almost unheard-of feat in those days of stay-at-home defensemen. The NHL of Shore's day was a rough-and-tumble league, in which defensemen were either made of iron, or had short careers. Eddie was one of the former: he played 14 seasons, and took more than 900 stitches. A model for modern medicine, Shore suffered just about every injury the human body could endure, and still arrived on time and ready to lead his Bruins. His nights in Boston and on the circuit were filled with pain and punishment. Shore had his nose broken 14 times, his jaw broken five times, broke his hip, back and collarbone, his eyes were damaged, his fingers were gnarled from repeated smashing, and he never needed to call on the dentist to have his teeth removed; his dentists wore colorful jerseys and carried hockey sticks.

The stories of Eddie Shore's remarkable strength and endurance abound, as do the tales of his peculiarities. He gave advice to anyone who would listen: He rubbed his stitches to keep his face baby smooth, he instructed his fellows to "stay away from your wife" or "part your hair on the other side" to get out of slump. His medical advice is legendary, though none of it would be found in the profes-

sional journals of his, or any other, day.

Shore played the game with incredible abandon; he would rush up the ice with such speed and determination that none dared to cross his path when he was at full stride. He patented the shoot and scoot game so often seen in today's hockey. He would shoot the puck against the backboards with such velocity that he would be there to retrieve it before the opposition could say "shot wide." Once in control of the puck in the offensive zone, he would flick a backhander to his teammates and block the defense while his pals packed the puck behind the befuddled goaltender.

It was this sense of complete abandon that led Shore to be remembered as the antagonist in one of hockey's most infamous incidents. In a game against the Toronto Maple Leafs on December 12, 1933, Eddie Shore hit Toronto's Ace Bailey from behind with such a force that Bailey landed square on his head. The sickening thud could be heard from ice to rafters, and Bailey's life was in the balance for several days. The following February 14 the NHL held the first All-Star Game ever, for the benefit of Ace Bailey, whose career was over. An Ace–Eddie handshake, the roar of the crowd, and the Bailey–Shore incident came to a close. There were no hard feelings or regrets, that's just the way the game was played.

Were Eddie Shore only strong, determined and ferocious, he would be known as one of the greats of the game. But Shore was also smart. He had his peculiarities, to be sure, but his superior intuitions always kept him one step ahead of the pack; thus it is that Eddie Shore is one of the foremost superstars of the game.

CHARLIE CONACHER

TUNE IN - **GENERAL MOTORS HOCKEY BROADCASTS** *from* **COAST** *to* **COAS**

When Charles William Conacher came up to play for the Toronto Maple Leafs in 1929, he gave the crowd a taste of what was to come. In his first game the 19-year-old Toronto native found the net, and he added 19 more before the summer holidays.

In the following season he outscored all National League scorers, and in 1932, led the powerful squad to the Stanley Cup. The "Big Bomber" was to win the NHL scoring title on five occasions, and he took the Art Ross Trophy twice. During his nine-year stay with the Leafs they won the Cup once, and the league championship twice. They often say of big goal-scorers that they have soft hands, and in Conacher's case, this was true. Though he outscored most of his contemporaries in many of his Leaf seasons, he did so while losing time to an infected hand in 1930, and a broken hand in 1931, 1932 and 1936. Combined with his several shoulder dislocations and problems with his feet, one can only wonder what he might have done were he whole and sound throughout his career.

Charlie Conacher is best remembered as a member of that most venerable of Maple Leaf forward assemblies: the Kid line of Busher Jackson, Joe Primeau and Conacher. This line of young blood scored at will, and were the most fearsome trio of their time. In the 1930s it was a common sight to see Primeau set the table, and Conacher enjoy the feast. Busher Jackson can best be described as a jack-of-all-trades, setting up and scoring goals with equal dexterity. In the Stanley Cup-winning year of 1931-32, Jackson, Primeau and Conacher finished 1, 2 and 4 in the scoring race.

By 1938 Conacher's heyday was finished, and he went to Detroit for a season, and finally to New York where he played defense with Eddie Shore for the Americans. In later years (from 1947 to 1950), he would coach the Chicago Black Hawks.

One of the great family of Ontario athletes, he is remembered as a five-time All-Star left winger, the winner of two Art Ross Trophies, and a member of the Hockey Hall of Fame, into which he was inducted in 1961.

MAURICE RICHARD

Goaltenders around the National Hockey League between 1942 and 1960 all knew what to expect when they visited the Forum. And although they may have known what to expect, they could never prepare for the flash of his eyes, the blur of the Bleu, Blanc et Rouge, and the two sounds most associated with Maurice Richard – the smack of wood slapping rubber, and the roar of the crowd.

He was the consummate superstar. Early in his career he set what has become the most important single-season achievement in the game. On March 18, 1945, "the Rocket" scored his 50th goal in his 50th game of the season, and the hockey world was stupefied. Richard became an instant international sporting hero, and although he never reached that mark again, the pace was set for hockey players from that day to this.

Richard racked up numbers, to be sure, but it was not just that he scored goals and made plays that put him in front of the pack. His unblinking focus on the game is evident to anyone who has ever even seen his photograph. His intense concentration on the ice gave him trouble in the penalty box, but it seldom stopped him from appearing in the top ranks of the marksmen around the league. In his 978 career games, he scored 544 goals, assisted on 421 others, and spent more than 21 hours in the sin bin.

Richard commanded the respect of the entire sporting world, but in his hometown, he was a legend. So powerful was Richard's influence in Montreal that when he was suspended in 1955 for hitting an official, the people of Montreal went crazy. In response to NHL President Clarence Campbell's decision to suspend Richard, the fans took to the streets, generally making a shambles of St. Catherine Street until their hero took the airwaves and appealed for an end to the riot.

In five different seasons, Richard scored more goals than any other player. In his 18 years in the big leagues, he only missed being the All-Star right winger four times, and his playoff performances are legend. His 15 post-season appearances brought him eight Stanley Cup rings. When he hung up the blades after the 1960 campaign, they didn't wait three years, they just put him in the Hall of Fame. A legend of the game whose magic will never be forgotten, Maurice Richard is one of the brightest lights in the hockey universe.

Opposite: *Maurice "Rocket" Richard reads the names of the famous and infamous who scratched their signatures inside the ancient "grail" of hockey. Richard and the Canadiens had just defeated the Boston Bruins to become the 1958 Stanley Cup champions.*

Right: *Richard poses with the puck he used to set a new high-water mark with his 400th NHL goal in December of 1954.*

Below: *Continuing his bid to shatter all the records, Richard displays the puck and stick he used to score his 600th goal (including playoffs) in November of 1958.*

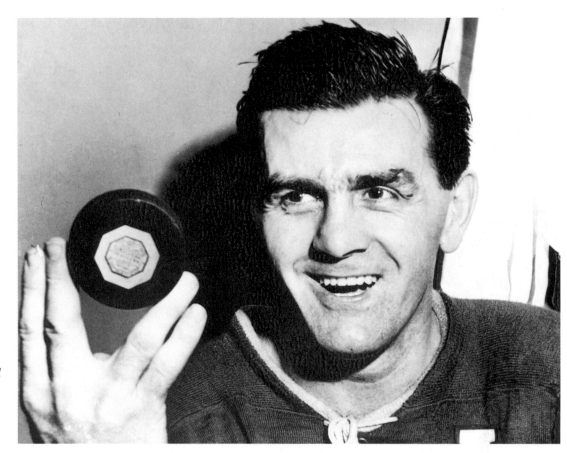

DOUG HARVEY

Left: *Doug Harvey was not a goal scorer, but he was the greatest defensive defenseman of all time.*

Opposite: *Doug Harvey played his finest years for the Montreal Canadiens, from 1947 to 1961. By the time he was sold to the New York Rangers, he was the owner of six Stanley Cup rings, and was the most respected blueliner in the game.*

When those who really know the game discuss the candidates for the all-time greatest defenseman, the name Doug Harvey is inevitably among those on the short list. In the defensive defensemen category though, there is no competition: Doug Harvey was simply the best.

The game has changed pretty radically since Harvey was patrolling the bluelines; he might look out of place in today's high-scoring game, where 12- and 14-goal games are the norm. When Harvey was the game's outstanding defenseman, the opposition was having a really good night if they managed three goals. In the 1950s, when Harvey had his best years, his Montreal Canadiens averaged slightly more than 155 goals against per season.

This kind of average was by no means the standard around the league, but it was the kind of play that developed out of a team which packed the likes of Maurice Richard, Jean Beliveau, Bert Olmstead, Jacques Plante and Doug Harvey.

Harvey was not a goal-scorer. In his 1,113 career games, he scored only 88 times, and never reached 10 in a year. Harvey's role was that of team quarterback. He was able to control the flow of the game, and pick up the pace or slow things down as was required by the situation. Doug Harvey knew what he was doing behind the blueline: he had some of the best marksmen in the game in front of him, one of the

game's most decorated goaltenders behind him, and his determination kept the likes of Gordie Howe, Alex Delvecchio, Johnny Bucyk, Bobby Hull and Frank Mahovlich from padding their statistics in Montreal. He often figured in the scoring, making sensational passing plays, and setting up his forward squad 452 times in his regular-season career.

In his 14 years with the Habs, Harvey skated on Stanley Cup ice thirteen times, six times winning the big silver bowl. In 1952 he was appointed to the first All-Star team, and did not relinquish the spot on the roster until seven seasons had passed. In all, he was appointed to this exulted team 10 times in his 19 years.

The real mark of Doug Harvey's superstar stature is found in his James Norris Memorial Trophies. Sportswriters around the hockey scene vote for this trophy, and in the days when legends of the game like Red Kelly, Tim Horton, Harry Howell and Bill Gadsby were alive and skating behind the bluelines of big league rinks, Doug Harvey was the consistent choice for best defenseman in the NHL. He was the Norris Trophy-winner four successive times, from 1955 to 1958, and another three consecutive times from 1960 to 1962.

Doug Harvey, an intelligent, clean playmaker, and a solid, stalwart playbreaker, is surely one of the true superstars of the game of hockey.

BERNIE GEOFFRION

When Maurice Richard scored 50 goals in 50 games, Bernie Geoffrion was still a kid, smacking his puck against a brick wall and dreaming of the day when he might practice his new shot against real, big-time goaltenders. As a pretty good hockey player, he probably believed that he might one day make it to the Forum, but he could never have dreamed that he would be the second man to reach 50 goals in a season.

Geoffrion broke into the NHL with another superstar, Jean Beliveau, and in his first game, against the New York Rangers, he potted his first goal. He was a fiery tempered right winger, and he let it be known that he would not be trifled with. As a young star with the best team in hockey, he had his work cut out for him and he made his first mark by winning the Calder Memorial Trophy in his first season as a regular with the squad.

Geoffrion had an ace up his sleeve. Since his days behind the garage, he had been practicing a new technique. Goal-scorers before him had done their job by flicking the puck with their wrists, but Geoffrion had found that with practice, he could bring his stick way up high behind him and smack it down on the puck, thereby increasing the velocity tremendously. Now that he had real big-time goaltenders to practice on, he tried out the shot in scrimmages and drills, much to the surprise of the jittery men who faced them. At first, the players thought it was kind of funny, and coach Dick Irvin was reluctant to set him loose with the shot in a real game, but once the shot had struck fear into the hearts of some of the coolest plumbers in the league, Irvin was silenced, and the men who laughed and called him "Boom-Boom" began to practice "the shot."

"Boomer," as they came to call him, won the scoring title in 1955, and though Richard was still the first-string right winger for the Habs, even the Rocket had to spend some time on the bench, watching Geoffrion climb the scoring ladder. He slapped his way through the middle years of the decade, only once falling short of the 20-goal mark, and he ushered in the 1960s with 50 goals in the season. Coupled with 45 assists, his record-tying mark was crowned with the Art Ross Trophy, the mark of the NHL's scoring championship, and the Hart Trophy as the league's MVP.

In a playing career which spanned 16 years, Boomer made the post-season 16 times, and was a big part of six Cup winners. He was a member of three All-Star squads in the days when Gordie Howe, Maurice Richard and Andy Bathgate made their names skating up the right wing. The inventor and formidable user of one of the most consequential developments in the game since the forward pass, Geoffrion has earned his way into the Hall of Fame.

Left: *Best known as the Habitant who invented the slap-shot, Boom-Boom Geoffrion looks a little uncomfortable here, playing against his former teammate, Jacques Plante.*

Opposite top: *Bernie Geoffrion scores his third goal of the night in the third game of 1955 Stanley Cup finals, leading the Canadiens to a 4-2 win over the Red Wings. Detroit goalie Terry Sawchuk can only look back in dismay.*

Opposite bottom: *As Geoffrion raises his arms in triumph, Bruins skater Joe Watson lumbers in behind the play just in time to see the puck emerge from the Boston cage.*

TERRY SAWCHUK

Left: *Netminder Terry Sawchuk played in Toronto for three seasons, sharing the duties with Johnny Bower. In 1965 the duo combined to win Sawchuk's fourth Vezina Trophy.*

Opposite top: *Alan Stanley seems to think he has beaten Terry Sawchuk, but Sawchuk did not become one of the best in the game by letting through this sort of shot.*

Opposite bottom: *In 1959, after a quick stay in Boston, Sawchuk was back in the Detroit nets. Here Canadien Henri Richard's shot is deflected, and Sawchuk dives to cover the loose disk.*

Whether or not he was the greatest netminder to ever strap on the pads is a matter of debate, but one thing is certain: Terry Sawchuk compiled career statistics that will never be surpassed – lifetime marks that secure his place as a super-star in the game of hockey.

When the Detroit Red Wings brought up the Winnipeg, Manitoba, native late in the 1950 season they soon realized their problems between the pipes were over. Sawchuk had already won Rookie of the Year honors in both the United States Hockey League and the American Hockey League when the Wings gave him a full-time taste of life in the big leagues in 1951. Sawchuk immediately made a lasting impression on NHL marksmen by adding the Calder Memorial Trophy as NHL Rookie of the Year to his trophy shelf, and racking up a league high 11 shutouts. The following season he set standards that are still being chased by NHL puck-stoppers. Sawchuk led the loop in goals against average and shutouts, but that was just a preview of what was to come in the playoffs. In the 1952 post-season, Sawchuk won all eight games he played (four of them were shutouts), as the Wings cruised to Stanley Cup victories in 1954 and 1955. He was rewarded in 1956 with a trade to Boston, a team that hadn't tasted Cup champagne since 1941. His stay in Beantown was brief and when the Wings skated onto the ice to start the 1957-58 campaign, Sawchuk was once again the team's Number 1 cage plumber.

After another seven seasons in Detroit, Sawchuk was sent to Toronto where he teamed up with Johnny Bower to win his fourth Vezina Trophy in 1965.

In 1967 the Leafs went to the Cup finals for the first time in three seasons, largely riding on the coattails of the venerable Sawchuk, who single-handedly shut down the engines of the Golden Jet and the rest of the Chicago Black Hawks in the semifinals. Sawchuk rose to the Stanley Cup occasion one more time, and when the ice was cleared after the Toronto–Montreal final, the Leafs had won their 11th Cup pennant, largely on the merits of Mr. Sawchuk.

By this time Sawchuk was 38 years old, and although he hung on to play until 1970, his days of glory were over. At the end of the 1970 campaign, a freak accident happened that eventually ended the life of one of the greatest players to ever guard the crease. In his two decades in the NHL, Sawchuk shut out his opponents a record 103 times, a mark that will never be broken. He won four Vezina Trophies, had only two seasons in which his GAA rose above 3.00, and had at least one shutout in 20 of his 21 seasons guarding the cage. The Hockey Hall of Fame saluted this superstar of the game by waiving the usual waiting period and inducting Terry Sawchuk to a well-deserved place of honor among the heroes of hockey in 1971.

JACQUES PLANTE

It is common knowledge that Jacques Plante pioneered the goaltender's face mask, and all who followed him owe him a great debt; but the invention of the face mask was by no means his only contribution to the game. His list of achievements is as lengthy as his 19 years in the big leagues.

Plante made the Montreal Canadiens' big club in 1952 – 53, and the next year became the team's Number 1 netminder. From the beginning, it was clear that he was a different sort of goaltender. He was an innovator right from the start: Jacques Plante was not satisfied to play the game from his 6-by 4-foot cage. He insisted on roaming around the defensive zone, doing everything in his power to gain the advantage. He would skate around behind his net and flop on the loose puck, freezing the play until the whistle called for a face-off. The NHL brass got wise to Plante's ploy, and introduced a rule to disallow his control of the play. Since he was no longer allowed to freeze the puck, Plante would leave his crease to either stop the puck for his defensemen, or fire it up to the forward squad, often finding Richard, Beliveau or Geoffrion to receive his crisp passes. Today, this is expected of a goaltender, but in Plante's day, it was his unique style.

On November 2, 1959, Plante got his face in the way of an Andy Bathgate backhander, and appeared 20 minutes later with the greatest hockey innovation since the tube skate: his now-famous fiberglass face mask.

It was a testimony to the superstar status of Plante that management allowed him to continue to wear the mask. The debates raged among coaches, managers, fans and players alike, each having his own opinion on whether the mask was a help or a visual hindrance. When the Montreal Canadiens went unbeaten in 11 games with Plante wearing the mask, the detractors were silenced.

It was not his technical innovations which made Jacques Plante a superstar, however; it was his performance between the pipes that earned him his berth in the Hockey Hall of Fame. He won six Vezina Trophies with the Montreal Canadiens, and led the league in shutouts four times. The Habs rewarded him by first dispatching him to the minors, and later trading him to the New York Rangers. Plante retired in 1965, but when the league expanded in 1967, he suited up with the St. Louis Blues, where he added another Vezina Trophy to his lengthy list of achievements. St. Louis sold him to Toronto, where at the age of 41, he registered the second lowest goals against average of his career, an astounding 1.88. He moved on to Boston and later to Edmonton of the World Hockey Association, where he ended his playing days.

In his 19 years in the bigs, Plante racked up 82 regular-season shutouts and added 14 more in the playoffs. He was an All-Star six times, and won the Hart Trophy as the league's Most Valuable Player in 1962. Jacques Plante, one of the most important men to ever don the pads, died on February 27, 1986.

Opposite: *Jacques Plante is held aloft by teammates Phil Goyette, Dollard St. Laurent, and Guy Talbot after backstopping the Habs to Stanley Cup victory over the Bruins in 1957.*

Above: *Plante struggles to keep the puck out of the cage during 1955 Stanley Cup finals action, as Doug Harvey interferes with Red Wing Ted Lindsey.*

Right: *Plante explains the principles behind his latest facial creation in 1970.*

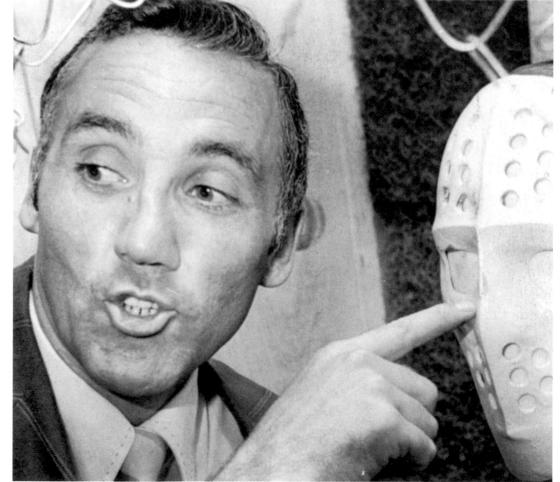

JEAN BELIVEAU

When Jean Beliveau joined the Montreal Canadiens for the 1953-54 season, he was one of the most heralded rookies of all time. A huge star with the Quebec Aces of the Quebec Senior League, Beliveau had been up for a few games in the previous two seasons. The Habs knew what to expect of him and they signed him to an unheard of $100,000, five-year contract.

It didn't take Beliveau long to stake out his ground as a team leader, and by the time he was made team captain in 1961, he was already a hockey legend. In his third season, he scored 47 goals, good for first place in the scoring race, and was also awarded the Hart Trophy as the league's Most Valuable Player.

The following season began that dream-like period for the Montreal club when they won five consecutive Stanley Cups. Beliveau figured big in all these post-season outings, scoring 28 goals and assisting in 27 others in those remarkable playoffs. "Le Gros Bill," as he was nicknamed, strung together 16 uninterrupted post-season appearances and a total of 17 in his 20 seasons. The reward for these 17 attempts was 10 Stanley Cup rings.

Beliveau was a steady skater, a giant strider who was very difficult to slow down, and nearly impossible to move out of the slot. He registered 13 seasons of 20-plus goals, and in his 1,125 regular season games totalled 507 goals, 712 assists, and finished his career with 1,219 points. His playoff records show what he was really made of, however: in 162 games he scored 79 goals and 97 assists for a post-season total of 176, an average of 10 points per appearance.

These numbers are impressive, but the important thing about his scoring wasn't how many, but rather, when. In one out of every twelve games in which he appeared, it was a Beliveau goal that took the game; he scored a career 80 game-winning goals.

At 6'3", 205 pounds, "Big Jean" carried his superstar stature as few others before or since have managed. He was a hero, to be sure, but he was also the consummate role model. As elegant off the ice as on, Beliveau could have become Prime Minister of Canada just as easily as a hockey superstar. He was always ready with a smile, a handshake, or an encouraging word to an autograph-seeking youngster.

In 1971 Beliveau skated into retirement and directly into the Hall of Fame; so clear was his place among the greats of the game that they waived the waiting period, and inducted him right away. The winner of two Hart Trophies as the NHL's Most Valuable Player, recipient of the first Conn Smythe Trophy as the playoffs' most important player and a member of nine All-Star teams, Jean Beliveau will always be counted as one of the superstars of hockey.

Below: *Jean Beliveau stuffs his 500th goal behind Minnesota's Gilles Gilbert.*

Opposite above: *Beliveau (#4) stops on a dime to confuse the rival Leafs.*

Opposite below: *Beliveau pours Stanley Cup champagne in 1965.*

JOHNNY BOWER

Punch Imlach, coach and general manager of the Toronto Maple Leafs from 1958 to 1969, once described goaltender Johnny Bower as "the best athlete in the world and I don't care if anybody wants to argue it." This is a rare commendation from the tough-minded Imlach, who would rather denounce a player than laud his abilities. In the case of Johnny Bower, no praise is strong enough to describe his courage and determination.

Known as the "China Wall" during his playing days, both for his ability to stonewall the opposition and for his age, Bower shuffled around the minor leagues for eight years before finally getting a shot at the big time. In 1953-54 the New York Rangers promoted him from their Cleveland farm club, and although he played a full season with the Broadway Blues, he was returned to the minors the following year. Instead of bemoaning his fate, Bower accepted his demotion by being selected as the Western Hockey League's best goaltender. He continued to shine in the minors, moving from Vancouver to Cleveland to Providence, racking up awards and All-Star nominations at every stop. Just when it appeared that Bower was destined to spend his final playing days riding the buses in the bush leagues, Imlach took over the reins of the faltering Toronto Maple Leaf team. Imlach's first move was to claim Bower off the waiver wire and give the 34-year-old veteran the opportunity he had waited 15 years to receive.

Imlach made Bower his number 1 goaltender, and the "China Wall" responded by guiding the resurrected Leaf team to four Stanley Cup titles. Bower led all NHL goaltenders in goals against average on three occasions and captured the Vezina Trophy, emblematic of the league's best netminder, twice. When he finally hung up the pads during the 1969-70 season, he was 45 years old. In 1976 Bower received his greatest honour when he was selected as a distinguished member of the Hockey Hall of Fame.

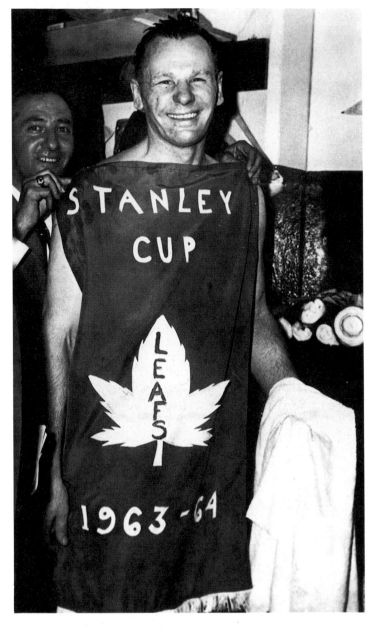

Above: *Leaf goalie Johnny Bower wears a Stanley Cup banner and a victory smile after Toronto defeated the Red Wings on April 26, 1964, to win the cup for the third straight time.*

Left: *Johnny Bower takes Detroit's Gordie Howe (9) out of action in the 1963 Stanley Cup finals.*

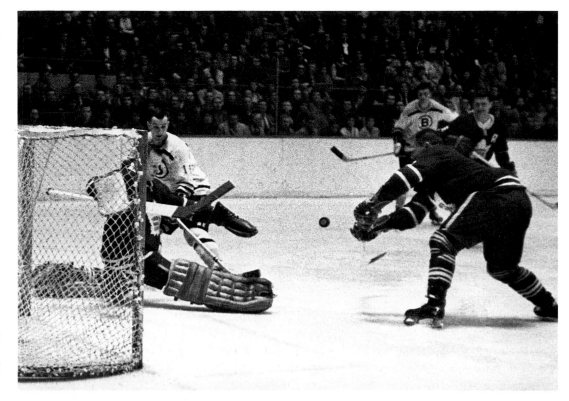

Right: *Johnny Bower's well-timed kick save prevents a goal by the Bruins' offense in 1964 game action.*

Below: *Johnny Bower and teammate Tim Horton are poised for Gordie Howe's shot in 1962 game action. Bower, a two-time Vezina Trophy winner, was elected to the Hall of Fame in 1976.*

GLENN HALL

"Mr. Goalie," as they call him in the record books, came up with the Detroit organization in 1956. He'd been up for coffee a few times in the previous two years, but with Terry Sawchuk as the key pipe man at Olympia Stadium, he was best kept in abeyance until he was ready.

In 1955-56, he was ready. The rookie stumped a parade of household names from scoring on the Red Wings, and finished the season with a 2.11 average, just behind his counterpart in Montreal, Jacques Plante. Hall won the Calder Trophy as the NHL's best rookie, and the confidence it gave him kept him in 552 consecutive hockey games. For the next six years he would not miss a single game, reminding the old-timers of an earlier iron man of the net, Georges Vezina.

In 1957 Hall was dispatched to Chicago in a trade which involved Hall and Ted Lindsay for some promising talent which did not pan out for the Wings. Chicago was happy to have Hall. His two years in the NHL had yielded a Rookie of the Year Award, a league-leading shutout high of 12, and more games won than any other goalie in the 1956-57 season. Chicago's new team workaholic continued to do yeoman service toiling in their nets. He continued to play without relief and to turn in fantastic performances. Chicago was not a powerhouse during Hall's nine-year stay there, but between Hall's relentless foiling and Bobby Hull's consistent scoring, they managed the one Stanley Cup which will suffice them both.

By the time Hall arrived in Chicago, he had already played 15 games in the post-season, and over the course of his career he would play 115 games in 15 spring campaigns. He once registered a 2.1 goals against average, and twice led all post-season plumbers in shutouts. In 1968, when age should have demanded that his career wind down, Hall was picked up by an expansion team in the draft, and he went on to play some of his most memorable hockey. The St. Louis Blues had only just entered the league, and the goaltending champion Hall brought the ragtag assembly of veterans and inexperienced puck-slingers into Stanley Cup final play. The Series went to the Habs in four straight, but so phenomenal was Hall's league-leading 1,111 minutes of post-season play that year, that he was awarded the Conn Smythe Trophy as the playoffs' Most Valuable Player.

Glenn Hall was not a headline grabber. He was the kind of hockey player who was best appreciated by those who faced his gridlock, and by coaches who knew the value of steady, cool play. Over his long career he played in 906 games, winning 407, and tying 165. His career average is a remarkable 2.51, and he registered 84 shutouts in his 18 years. An All-Star 11 times, Hall put his name on the Vezina Trophy three times, and entered the Hall of Fame in 1975.

Opposite: *Chicago's iron man netminder, Glenn Hall shows his talent outside the crease, challenging Montreal's Claude Larose. An 11-time All-Star, Hall played during his long and prolific career for Detroit, Chicago and St. Louis, hanging up his blades in 1971.*

Right: *Glenn Hall enjoys a cool drink in the locker room after Chicago's 3-1 victory over his former Red Wing teammates in the 1961 Stanley Cup finals.*

Below: *Hall is not counting on his teammate Jack Evans to look after the bouncing puck as he tried to knock it away before the Leafs' Bob Pulford gets a blade on it. The durable and talented goalie was elected to the Hall of Fame in 1975.*

BOBBY HULL

Through the 1950s the Chicago Black Hawks had been the perennial cellar dwellers of the National Hockey League, finishing last in the loop for four years running, but when Bobby Hull joined the lineup for the 1957-58 season, this was about to change. As a rookie, Hull had a reasonably good year, scoring 47 points in the 70-game season, but he was, after all, a rookie. It wouldn't take long before this strong and handsome bull from Point Anne, Ontario, would revolutionize the National Hockey League.

Two seasons later, when the curtain closed on the 1960 campaign, Bobby Hull had finished the year with more goals than any other big-league marksman, scoring 39 markers. His 42 assists put him over the top, and Hull became the first Art Ross Trophy winner of the decade. It was the beginning of a string of major sporting achievements for Hull, but more than that, it was the start of a love affair be-

tween "the Golden Jet" and the hockey world.

Hull was superstar material from the start. He had the chiselled features of a movie star, an almost boyish charm when interviewed or photographed, and he put on a show like nobody on the ice circuit. Although he did not invent the slap shot, his use of it revolutionized the game. It was not just that his shot was hard – though it was estimated at upwards of 120 miles per hour – the legend of his slap shot is that it was absolutely accurate. No other player has mastered the ability to smack the rubber "where the goalie ain't" like Hull, and the videotapes of his impressive use of the new technique are still valuable learning tools for today's big league shooters.

When in 1961-62 Hull joined that small and celebrated group of men who had scored 50 goals in a season, defensemen around the league were put on notice. Their job when playing Chicago would be to stop this guy at any cost. He was now a two-line scoring champion, and had brought the Hawks from the basement of the league to the Stanley Cup winner's circle. He was the man to watch for.

In 1966 Bobby Hull raised the stakes for NHL scorers. In that season, he first tied, then obscured the previous high-water mark of 50 goals in a campaign, when he scored his 51st goal in a memorable tilt against the New York Rangers. He finished the season with 54 goals and 96 points and headed for the awards ceremonies assured of his third championship Art Ross Trophy.

Hull's one Stanley Cup came early in his career, but his individual ability continued to make an impact on the regular- and post-season results for years. From 1959 until he left the league in 1972, Hull's Hawks missed the post-season only once, and although they never skated with the Cup aloft again, the taste of victory kept the men skating and the fans cheering for years.

Though he was the darling of the National Hockey League, and still among the best sharpshooters in the loop, Hull was having contract troubles with the Hawks' management. He knew he was worth more money than they were prepared to give him, and with an offer on the table from the upstart World Hockey Association, Hull decided to take the money and run. The Golden Jet became a Winnipeg Jet, and the fortunes of that renegade league changed instantly. The acquisition of Hull gave the new loop the leverage they needed to become a real force in hockey, and many other NHLers followed his lead into the big money. Hull continued his high-scoring game, registering his highest point total, 77 goals and 65 assists, while in Winnipeg.

Hull moved back to the NHL when the WHA merged with their former rivals, and he played his final series with Gordie Howe and the Hartford Whalers.

The legacy of Bobby Hull is among the most formidable on the books. He scored a career 913 goals, 895 assists, and 1,908 points, had five NHL seasons with 50 or more goals, was the league's Most Valuable Player in 1965 and 1966, was the league's most gentlemanly player in 1965, was selected to 12 All-Star teams, and had a career 28 hat tricks. Bobby Hull, handsome, roguish, rugged and prolific, skated into the Hockey Hall of Fame after 23 years at the top of the charts in the world's fastest sport. Today, he is among the proudest of fathers, to see his son, "the Golden Brett" carving his name in the modern day record books, and following the trail of glory.

Opposite: *Hull shows off his 400th and 401st NHL goal pucks, on January 7, 1968.*

Right: *The Golden Jet (#9) hugs teammate Pat Stapleton after firing his record-breaking 51st goal of the season in the third period of this late-season match in 1966.*

Overleaf: *Hull beats Ranger Brad Park to the disk in this 1971 matchup. Hull combined strength, speed and determination to lead his Hawks through 15 seasons, missing the post-season on only two occasions. The Ranger on the left, looking for all the world like Darryl Sittler, and wearing number 27, is in fact Ted Irvine.*

GORDIE HOWE

There are stars and there are superstars, and then there is Gordie Howe. Simply put, Gordie Howe was the most consistently excellent player the game has ever known. In the encyclopedia there is no nickname listed for this most celebrated of ice heroes, but the entire world knows him as "Mr. Hockey."

In hockey, a man who has played in the bigs for more than a few years is considered a veteran. In the fast-paced bumping and bruising world known as the National Hockey League, more than a handful of seasons is more than most men can take. Twenty-year men are uncommon, and those who manage that number are generally the stars of the game. Gordie Howe played 32 years of big league hockey, and in his final year played the full schedule of 80 games and scored a respectable 41 points.

As a child in Floral, Saskatchewan, Gordie Howe, like every other kid, idolized the names they heard over the radio, and the faces which stared out at them from the

sports pages of the local papers. His dream of hockey stardom came somewhat closer when a neighbor gave Gordie his first skate. He didn't get a pair; the other one was for his sister, but it didn't take long before she gave up, and he had the pair for the pond. The rest, as they say, is history.

He came up with the Wings in 1946, and never looked back. Although his first three seasons were nothing more than respectable, by the end of the fourth it was abundantly clear that Detroit had somebody special wearing number 9. Using his stick to push pucks and his elbows to make room, Howe was considered one of the toughest offensive players in the game. Gordie Howe was not a Montreal Canadien,

and although his hometown fans were not born and raised in the place of hockey's birth, the Detroit Red Wings and the Detroit fans certainly knew how to appreciate their superstar. Gordie Howe was the toast of Motown. He was the kind of player any city could love, but he was just what the Detroit faithful loved about hockey – he was tough, fast, and was not above a confrontation. Though Gordie was never in the running for the penalty race, nobody ever accused him of gunning for the Lady Byng Memorial Trophy.

It is difficult to talk about the "prime" of Gordie Howe, as it seems to elude us as surely as his retirement eluded him. He won the scoring race fives times in the 1950s and again in

There is Gordie Howe, then there are all the rest. One of the most dominant players in the history of the game, Howe has branded his name into the books like few other skaters ever have, or ever will. During his 26 NHL seasons – the most ever played by one man – Howe was appointed to 21 All-Star teams. Here Toronto netminder Ed Chadwick tries to keep an eye on both the puck and the man.

Opposite: *Mr. Hockey finished his career in 1980 with the Hartford Whalers of the NHL. His jump to the rogue WHA – where he played with the Houston Aeros and the New England Whalers – allowed him to play a season with his two sons. Rumor has it that he will return to play with his grandsons.*

Right: *This young Gordie Howe probably knew he was pretty good, but the down-to-earth farm boy could have had no idea what the future would hold for him. The most decorated man in the history of the game looks like any other youngster hoping to keep his place on the bench. The arm patch indicates the date of this photo: it was worn for the 1950-51 season.*

1963. He led the Detroit Red Wings through 26 seasons, and in his 23rd Red Wing year he peaked with a career high 103 points on the season.

Howe won four Stanley Cups with the Red Wings, all in the powerhouse days of the 1950s when he was teamed with Ted Lindsay and Sid Abel on the Production line. He played more years in the spring schedule than most men reach in the regular campaign, having played 235 games in 26 seasons. His points total for career post-season play are dramatic: 96 goals, 135 assists and 231 points, with 235 minutes in the penalty box.

If Howe had retired following his remarkable career in Detroit, he would have left records standing on the books for years to come. As it turned out, he took a couple of years off then signed up to play with the Houston Aeros of the WHA, where he realized his lifelong dream of playing with his sons, Mark and Marty. He remained in the WHA for six years, the only grandfather playing first division pro-

fessional ice hockey. He was an All-Star in the WHA several times, and jumped to the New England Whalers in 1977. When, in 1980, Gordie Howe finally retired from the ice, it was with an NHL club. His Whalers became the NHL's Hartford Whalers, and he finished his career playing with another noted number 9, the great Bobby Hull.

Since Gordie's retirement the game has changed radically, and the records of most of his contemporaries are recorded only in the minds of old-timers, but Gordie still has a few in the books. Among them are: most NHL seasons (26), most NHL games (1,767), most points by a right winger (1,850) and he is second only to the wunderkind, Wayne Gretzky, in NHL goals and in many of the assist categories. He was appointed to 21 NHL All-Star teams, was given the nod as the league's Most Valuable Player six times and led all NHL point-scorers in a half-dozen seasons. Simply put, Gordie Howe was the most consistently excellent player the game has ever known.

STAN MIKITA

Some athletes live with a public panache, and a ready word to the awaiting fans. Others save the drama for the game. Stan Mikita is one of the latter. Never one to go out of his way for public admiration, Stan Mikita never shirked the attention given him by his opponents.

Mikita had two very different careers in the National Hockey League. In his "first life," he was a sober ice lawyer, judge and executioner, who seemed to see it as his duty to punish those who would dare try to keep the puck in his end zone. They called him "le Petit Diable" (the little devil). If he had remained in this mold, he may have won the penalty race, but he would never have made it into the Hall of Fame.

Stan Mikita came up to the Chicago Black Hawks for the 1958-59 season, but did not become a regular with the club until the following season. He made his name as a tough guy in the league, and did that well. By 1963-64, he led the league in penalty minutes; a dubious title which was distinguished only because he also led the league in assists and in points. He was beginning to be name-brand player, winning the scoring race in 1964 and 1965, but it would take another season of scoring and bashing before he really came into his own.

In 1966-67, Mikita changed his game plan: he remained the league's leader in assists (62 assists), and in points (94 points), but he spent only 12 minutes in the sin bin, earning the Lady Byng Memorial Trophy for most gentlemanly player. He also won the Hart Trophy as the league's Most Valuable Player, and the Art Ross Trophy, as the league's leader in points. The following year he repeated his trifecta feat, becoming the first man to do so, and fixing his position as a true superstar of the game.

Mikita worked the edges of the game, looking for advantage where he could find it. In his early days, he established himself as a man not to be trifled with, and later, along with fellow "Scooter line" mate Kenny Wharram, he pioneered the curve-bladed hockey stick which characterized the 1960s. He found that this magic wand was a much more useful tool than were his fists.

Though his only Stanley Cup came early in his career (1961), Mikita's sharp passes kept the Hawks in the playoffs many times during his 16 years. His playoff performances were always solid; he scored 150 points in his 155 career post-season games. He was twice the league's Most Valuable Player, four times gathered more points than the league's best skaters, won two consecutive awards as the most gentlemanly player on ice, and represented the Chicago squad on the All-Star squad eight times. Stan Mikita, quiet, determined and unpredictable, is one of the reluctant superstars of the world's fastest sport.

FRANK MAHOVLICH

Left: *Frank Mahovlich brought strength, experience and heart to the Montreal Canadiens, where he played three and a half seasons, and took two Stanley Cups.*

Opposite top: *The Big M is one of three players to win multiple Cups with more than one team. The others are Red Kelly and Dick Duff.*

Opposite bottom: *No matter how many teams he played for, Mahovlich is still claimed as their own by a generation of Leaf fans. The blockbuster trade that sent Mahovlich to Detroit after 13 seasons in Toronto will be remembered as one of the darkest days in Leaf history.*

One of the more enduring images of the 1960s is that of Frank Mahovlich in full flight; picking up a pass at center, gliding effortlessly over the blueline and firing the cannonading shot that put fans in the seats and fear in the eyes of opposing goaltenders. The Big "M" connected on more than 500 of those blasts in his 18-year career, and received the ultimate tribute, induction into the Hockey Hall of Fame, in 1981.

Francis William Mahovlich was born January 10, 1938, in Timmins, Ontario, where he demonstrated early an uncanny ability to pop the pill in the net. He moved to southern Ontario where he starred with the St. Michael's Majors of the Ontario Hockey Association Junior A League, prompting an invitation to skate with the Toronto Maple Leafs in a three-game trial in 1957. Mahovlich impressed the Leaf brass and after they rewarded him with a contract, he rewarded them by winning the Calder Memorial Trophy in 1958. His star continued to rise when he potted 48 goals in 1961, and in 1962 led the Maple Leafs to their first Stanley Cup in 11 years.

Mahovlich reached true superstar status in October 1962 when Jim Norris, owner of the Chicago Black Hawks, offered $1 million for his services. The Leafs turned down the deal and Mahovlich was instrumental in the Toronto Buds winning four Stanley Cups in the sixties. In 1968, despite his numerous All-Star berths and eight 20-plus goal seasons, Mahovlich was deemed expendable by the Leafs and was dealt to Detroit in one of the decade's blockbuster trades. Mahovlich seemed reborn in Detroit and he turned in three productive campaigns for the Wings, but he was soon on the move again, this time to Montreal, where he sealed his career with some of his finest performances.

During his career Mahovlich was often misunderstood; he was by turns open and friendly, then moody and taciturn. The media and the fans always felt he could have done more, could have been so much better. However, his impressive statistics speak volumes about the man and his abilities: 533 goals, 1,103 career points spread over 18 NHL seasons, a nine-time All-Star and the proud winner of six Stanley Cup rings.

BOBBY ORR

Opposite and Right: The great Bobby Orr spent most of his abbreviated career with Boston, where he became the first NHL defenseman to win the league's scoring championship in 1969-70, and where he won the James Norris Memorial Trophy eight consecutive times as the league's top defenseman.

Overleaf: When Bobby Orr was whole and sound, there was nobody like him. His end-to-end rushes left crowds roaring and the opposition gasping for breath. Called by many the greatest player of all time, he certainly ranks among the superstars of the game.

In 1962 the Boston Bruins, a National Hockey League franchise for nearly 40 years, built its future around the promise of a 14-year-old kid from a backwater Ontario town. The kid was Bobby Orr, the town was Parry Sound, and the promise . . . well, let history speak for itself.

Orr was born in those heady days that followed World War II, when parents, flush with the promise the future would hold for their children, produced that big generation known as the "baby boomers."

Bobby, like so many great athletes, came by his talent honestly. His father, Doug, had been an excellent junior player, and Doug's father, Robert, was himself a professional athlete. Family influence played an important role in the story of this most remarkable of baby boomers. When Bobby was obliged to play in Oshawa at age 14, his father would drive him the three hours to and from games. Bobby was equally devoted to the family when the Bruins came to talk contract; the terms included new stucco for the family home, a second-hand car, or new clothes for the kids. This closeness would serve Bobby well when the dream turned to heartbreak.

Orr was just 18 years old when he scored his first goal in Boston Garden, receiving a three-minute standing ovation from the win hungry fans. Not only had the team pinned their hopes on this fresh-scrubbed kid, but so had the loyal fans of Causeway Street; they had made him a legend before his time.

The pressure on Bobby Orr was to work miracles. And work miracles he did. He spent the next 10 years setting high-water marks in virtually every category available. He was the first defenseman to score more than 40 goals, the

first player to gather more than 100 assists, the first defenseman to lead the pack in scoring, the first defenseman to score more than 100 points. Five times he led the league in assists. He won Rookie of the Year, two Art Ross Trophies, three Hart Trophies, eight consecutive James Norris Memorial Awards, two Stanley Cup rings, and he became the first man to win the Conn Smythe Trophy on more than one occasion. Bobby Orr, who lit up the ice when he skated, fulfilled his promise beyond the expectation of even the most zealous fan.

As with so many dreams, that of the great Number 4 began to melt into nightmare; despite recurrent knee problems, he played hard and fast, oblivious to pain and to the clear signals that something was dreadfully wrong. He was spending an inordinate amount of time looking up at the sober faces of medical doctors, and less and less time on the ice. By the age of 28, just 10 years after his debut in the big league, it was clear that this remarkable career would soon be over.

Orr was not prepared to accept the heartbreak of this defeat. In 1976 he went to play for the Chicago Black Hawks, where determination would not be enough. Bobby would play only 26 games over three seasons with the Hawks before hanging up the blades for keeps.

Amidst a near funereal backdrop, the legend of Bobby Orr moved from the rink to the boardroom. With the support and encouragement of his family, friends, fans and teammates, Orr overcame the trials of change to become successful as a businessman, a broadcaster, a father and a philanthropist. It is with great pride that the Hockey Hall of Fame includes Bobby Orr on its roster of greatness.

BERNIE PARENT

Left: *Bernie Parent turns away Ranger sniper Rod Gilbert. It took Bernie several years to find his place, but he finally settled down in Pennsylvania, where he led the Broadstreet Bullies to two Stanley Cups.*

Opposite: *This 1975 Stanley Cup final action sees Rene Robert and the Buffalo Bisons in their only final series appearance to date. In the six-game series, Parent and the Flyers limited the hot shots from the north to 12 goals in winning their second Cup.*

When the Philadelphia Flyers were building the team that would eventually become the first expansion club to win the Stanley Cup, they focused their attention on a young net-minder they spotted on the roster of the Boston Bruins. Although Bernard Michael Parent had shown promise in the Bruins' cage, he was left unprotected by Boston in the expansion draft of 1967 and the young Philadelphia club jumped at the chance to make the native of Montreal, Quebec, their Number 1 goaltender.

Parent quickly established himself as a steady puck-stopper who flourished under the heavy workload that was placed on his shoulders. In 1969-70, he appeared in 62 of the squad's 78 games, compiling a GAA of 2.79 and racking up 3 shutouts. The hockey world was shocked the following season when Parent was traded to the Toronto Maple Leafs, and though he continued to display his skills in the Leafs' net, his heart was clearly still in Philadelphia. Parent made headlines the next season as well, when he became one of the first "name" players to jump to the rival World Hockey Association, signing to play with the Philadelphia Blazers. When it was clear that Parent was not happy in the fledgling loop, he was set free, and he rejoined the Flyers for the 1973-74 campaign, just in time to solidify the Flyers' romp to the top of the NHL.

Playing with a new-found enthusiasm, Parent put to-

gether a pair of back-to-back Vezina Trophy-winning seasons in 1974 and 1975, becoming the first netminder since Jacques Plante to accomplish that feat. Parent, who led the NHL in victories and shutouts in each year, saved his finest performances for when it counted most: in the post-season. Parent played virtually every minute for Philly in the 1974 and 1975 playoffs, racking up 22 wins and 6 shutouts in these post-season parties. With Parent between the pipes, the Flyers cruised into the Stanley Cup winner's circle and in each case, it was Parent who guided the ship. In both 1974 and 1975, he won the deciding game of the Cup finals by posting a shutout, blanking the powerhouse Boston Bruins in 1974 and whitewashing the Buffalo Sabres in 1975. In recognition of his playoff heroics, Parent was awarded the Conn Smythe Trophy, and he remains the only performer to win that prestigious award two years in a row.

Bernie Parent continued to accumulate impressive statistics for the rest of his distinguished career, leading the league in victories once again in 1976, and finishing at the top of the NHL's shutout ladder in 1978. Although a freak eye injury prematurely ended his playing days in 1979, Parent continues to serve the Philadelphia organization as a goaltending instructor. The Hockey Hall of Fame inducted him in 1988, acknowledging his worthy place among the elites who have played the game of ice hockey.

PHIL ESPOSITO

Opposite: In a one-two squeeze that would leave lesser men out of the action, Espo (#7) pushes for that extra inch that set him aside from other young National Leaguers. Phil Esposito was known as one of the hardest workers to ever play in the NHL. He was not a great skater, so instead of finessing his way around the ice, he used his muscle. His powerful and accurate shot was a formidable weapon for the Black Hawks, Bruins and Rangers.

Right: Esposito debated long and hard whether he should give up his good job as a miner in Sudbury before accepting an offer to attend an NHL training camp. In the end, Espo gambled his two years of seniority in the mines to take a long shot at the game he loved. A member of the Hall of Fame and one of the best known names in the game today, Esposito is the proud owner of a new NHL franchise in Tampa Bay, Florida.

In 1967-68 the NHL was brimming with superstar caliber hockey players. The top ten scorers in this first year of expansion would all make the Hall of Fame. Most of the names were already established stars – Howe, Bucyk, Mikita, Hull – but there was a new star rising in the East, and Phil Esposito began to make his presence felt. He was about to launch a career that would see him break every existing single-season scoring record in the game.

Esposito grew up in the backwater town of Sault Ste. Marie, Ontario, and joined the Chicago Black Hawks in 1963. Although he had a fine touch around the net, he was often written off as a poor skater. Despite firing 27 goals for the Hawks in 1966, he was deemed expendable, and in the most written about trade in the history of the game to date, Esposito was dispatched, with Ken Hodge and Fred Stanfield, to Boston for three players, whose names were quickly forgotten. It was a move that would bring the Boston Bruins three Stanley Cups and the Chicago management nightmares.

"Espo" jelled in Boston, where he was allowed to play to his ability. A big man at 6'1", and 205 pounds, he planted himself in the slot and stayed there, bouncing off all defenders, and using his velvet touch to slip home the rubber.

He led the NHL in scoring in his second year in Beantown, and beginning in 1970, set standards for marksmen that would stand until a kid named Wayne came down the pond.

Esposito led the NHL in goals scored in six straight campaigns, including a 76-goal explosion in 1971, when he obliterated Bobby Hull's previous mark of 58 goals on the season. Espo won the Art Ross Trophy that year, and made a habit of leading the NHL in points, stringing together three more consecutive scoring championships.

Despite these high scoring numbers, Esposito didn't peak until Canada met the Soviet Union in 1972. After the fourth game of that series, he made an impassioned plea to the Canadian people, demanding that they make their voices heard in support of the pride of the great white north. Canadians heard the call of duty and Esposito did his valiant part. In the last two games of that historic series, Esposito scored five goals, and he returned to North America as a national hero.

Phil Esposito was the first National Leaguer to break the 100-point mark, he was an All-Star eight times, registered five 50-plus seasons, was the league's highest scorer five times, and with his remarkable scoring numbers, single-handedly ushered in the modern era of ice hockey.

BRAD PARK

Left: *Brad Park played 17 years in the NHL, and never missed the post-season. As fate would have it, however, he never clutched the Stanley Cup either. In a blockbuster trade he moved from New York to Boston in 1976, in exchange for Phil Esposito.*

Opposite: *Park shows his former Ranger mates what he did best, controlling the flow of the play.*

You won't find his name on the Stanley Cup, an injustice that broadly illustrates the frustrations of playing this game. Brad Park never missed the playoffs in his 17 years of skating in the NHL but, despite being one of the most talented rearguards to lace on the blades, he never found himself in the right place at the right time.

The New York Rangers stole the Toronto native right from under the noses of the Maple Leafs in 1966, and for the better part of eight seasons Brad Park's name was often mentioned just half a breath behind that of Bobby Orr. When Orr was lost to the Bruins because of a knee injury in 1975, Boston traded Phil Esposito to acquire Park, and he moved onto the Beantown blueline to replace the man who was a living legend in New England. Park didn't succumb to the pressure however, and he solidified the Boston defense for eight campaigns, leading the Bruins into the Cup finals in 1977 and 1978, and later tutoring a young Ray Bourque to take his place.

With seven All-Star nominations to his credit and 12 sea-

sons in which he scored 10 or more goals, Park certainly had superstar credentials. However, this performer had qualities that statistics cannot measure. Park had the unteachable ability to control the flow of the game, leading every team he played for into the post-season.

He proved himself a capable combatant if the situation called for it, often making sure that if he went to the sin bin, he took along a "buddy" from the opposing team.

During his career, Park was often overshadowed by the names Orr, Robinson and Potvin, but his career statistics are among the best of any NHL rearguard. He scored 213 goals on his way to racking up 896 total points, and in 1984 he was finally rewarded for his outstanding contributions to the game of hockey by winning the Masterton Trophy, awarded for perseverance and sportsmanship.

Although his name was never carved in the silver of Lord Stanley's mug, his name has been engraved in the honor roll of the Hockey Hall of Fame, a fitting testimony to his place as one of the superstars of the game of hockey.

BOBBY CLARKE

the Hart Trophy as the league's MVP, an award he received three consecutive times. He captained the first expansion team to win the Stanley Cup, and he was the first expansion player to break 100 points in a season. In his 1,144 games, he scored 1,210 points. The consummate playmaker, he led the NHL in assists on two occasions on his way to racking up 852 career helpers. As impressive as his offensive numbers are, it was the determination and hustle with which he played the game that put this pugnacious digger into the Hockey Hall of Fame.

If there was a goal that needed to be scored, if there was a pass that needed to be made, if there was a teammate who needed to be scolded or praised, Bobby Clarke came through in the clutch. He was often called the Dr. Jekyll and Mr. Hyde of ice hockey: the cool, confident playmaker could become a ferocious pugilist when the occasion demanded it. This was borne out in his penalty record: he spent more than 24 hours in the sin bin over his career, but rest assured, he seldom went in alone.

His Flyers, being an expansion team, were made up of very few finesse players. The ice was their battlefield, and they showed up game after game ready to go to the trenches, with Bobby Clarke often leading the attack. He started more than a few battles, but he was always there to finish them. He took Conn Smythe's credo to heart, "if you can't beat 'em in the alley, you can't beat 'em on the ice," and made it the motto for his own playbook. It worked for Smythe and his Leafs in the early days, and it worked for Clarke and the Flyers in the bash and clobber days of early NHL expansion. The Flyers took only two Stanley Cups, but once they found their stride in 1971-72, Clarke's bashing brethren never missed post-season play.

Bobby Clarke was not a natural superstar; greatness did not come easy to him. Clarke beat the odds through hard work, determination and head-on battles with adversity to become one of the superstars of hockey's modern age.

Robert Earle Clarke was born on August 13, 1949, in Flin Flon, Manitoba. He became the gut-busting hero of the Philadelphia Flyers who exemplified the winner-take-all "Broad Street Bullies" of the 1970s. He was the most fiercely competitive hockey player of his day; the original 110 percent man, and as his opponents would often say, he would do anything to win.

The fact that Bobby Clarke was even playing professional hockey says a lot about the man who would lead the Philadelphia Flyers to two Stanley Cup victories. When he was 15, it was discovered that the budding star was diabetic. Instead of letting the disease ruin his dreams, he used it as a constant hurdle to be overcome, a barrier he would continually vault.

Clarke was the first member of an expansion team to win

Opposite top: *Bobby Clarke poses for a publicity shot. The fiercely competitive three-time MVP captained the first expansion team – his Philadelphia Flyers – to win the Stanley Cup.*

Opposite below: *Bobby Clarke, the Flyers' feisty digger, was best known for his unbending determination and incredible endurance. Seen here in action against the now defunct Atlanta Flames, Clarke shows his control of the game by slowing down the opposition.*

Right: *Clarke flashes the grin of a great ice warrior: a dentist's dream, a mother's nightmare.*

Playoff heroes are often previously unheralded men. The history of the Stanley Cup is full of "nobodies" who come out and lead a team to victory. It is interesting to note that most of these bright lights in the playoff skies prove to be shooting stars, disappearing as rapidly as they appear. It is true that when Ken Dryden arrived on Stanley Cup ice for the 1971 playoffs he was a relative nobody, however it is anything but true to say that his stardom was fleeting.

Dryden arrived in the NHL for the last six games of Montreal's 1971 season. He was an All-American at Cornell University and had toiled between the pipes for Canada's National Team, but no one, including the experts, could have predicted his pivotal role in the greatest playoff series in living memory.

Dryden won all six regular-season games that he played for the Habs, which was surprising in itself, but when he skated out against the defending Cup Champion Bruins in the 1971 quarterfinals, fans and critics alike were in shock. Dryden played every minute of every game in that playoff series, and after he had turned away Esposito and Orr, and closed the door on Hull and Mikita in the finals, the Montreal Canadiens were among the most shocked and astounded at the steady play of this incredible backstopper. School boys across the nation imitated his characteristic stance, resting

his two arms on the butt of his goal stick, as he peered out anonymously from behind his mask.

Ken Dryden played only eight years in the NHL, but while he was there, he established himself as one of the game's greatest cage plumbers. Having taken the Conn Smythe Trophy as the playoffs' MVP for his performance the year before, he became the first man to win the Rookie of the Year after already having won a major NHL trophy. Dryden returned the Canadiens to the NHL winner's circle in 1973, the same year in which he won his first Vezina Trophy as the league's best goaltender. He then shocked the hockey world again, this time by retiring from the game to finish his law degree. The Canadiens came calling in 1974, this time with more money than he could reasonably refuse. Law degree in hand, he strapped on the tools of ignorance once again, and played his usual knowledgeable game. Although the Habs were kept out of the Stanley Cup finals in 1975, it was the last time that Dryden would miss drinking champagne from Lord Stanley's Silver Mug.

From 1976 to 1979, Ken Dryden was the most dominant player in the National Hockey League. He led the league in victories twice, shutouts three times, and goals against average on four consecutive occasions. The Montreal Canadiens, in these four years, needed only 19 games out of a possible 28 final-series matches to capture four Stanley Cups. In 1977 Ken Dryden lost only six games, and in his entire career he never lost more than ten games in any season. A six-time All-Star, member of the Hockey Hall of Fame, and one of the most articulate men who ever laced up skates, Ken Dryden is one of the greatest stars in the history of the game.

Opposite and below: *Ken Dryden in the Canadiens' net. No goaltender is so readily identifiable as is this hero of the hometown Habs, whose style was unique and whose achievements were many.*

Overleaf: *Ken Dryden did not lead the Montreal Canadiens to six Stanley Cups by letting the disk slip behind him. Here he deflects the puck in a game against the New York Rangers.*

GILBERT PERREAULT

Left: *Gilbert Perreault was the Buffalo franchise for 17 years. His career as a Sabre literally began with the spin of the wheel of fortune in 1970.*

Opposite: *Perreault is the only man on the "French Connection" line of Perreault, Richard Martin and Rene Robert to have made the Hall of Fame.*

Hockey men have always been gamblers, staking their professional careers on the talents of young skaters and looking for that one ace in the hole. It seems appropriate then, that when the executives of the Vancouver Canucks and Buffalo Sabres met on June 9, 1970, to decide who would have the first selection in the 1970 amateur draft, a carnival wheel was used to determine that fateful choice. With a spin of the wheel of fortune, the Sabres won and they chose Gil Perreault as the man to lead their new squad into the NHL wars.

For 17 seasons Gil Perreault was the "Franchise" for the Buffalo side, leading the team on the ice and in the dressing room. Perreault was an instant hit with the Buffalo faithful: he had the smooth moves of a Jean Beliveau, the instincts of a Stan Mikita, and the scoring touch of a Jean Ratelle. In his rookie campaign, Perreault set new standards for NHL freshmen by firing home 38 goals, an accomplishment that earned him the Calder Memorial Trophy. As he matured, so did his youthful teammates. When he was placed on a line with Rick Martin and Rene Robert, the Sabres and Perreault were ready to scale new heights. In 1975 this high-powered "French Connection" combination led Buffalo into the Stanley Cup finals, the only time the Sabres have come

that close to sipping champagne from the vaunted Mug.

Perhaps the finest attribute of Perreault's game was his consistency. Although he scored 20 or more goals in 15 different seasons in the NHL, Perreault preferred to share the spotlight with his teammates by delivering deadly accurate passes to their sticks and allowing them to fire home key markers. A check of the statistical chart shows the great Gil had 15 campaigns in which he set up more goals than he scored, a lofty accomplishment when one considers that he took the opportunity to score 512 goals himself, a mountain scaled by only 15 men in NHL history.

Perreault holds or shares 10 individual records for the Sabres, including goals, assists, games, seasons and points. He was a two-time All-Star and the worthy recipient of the Lady Byng Memorial Trophy in 1973, when he spent a mere 10 minutes in the cooler. On September 24, 1990, Gilbert Perreault was honored for his on-ice excellence with his induction into the Hockey Hall of Fame. A further honor befitting a superstar of his caliber was delivered on October 17, 1990. On that autumn evening, Perreault's Number 11 jersey was retired by the Sabres and hung from the rafters in the Memorial Auditorium, securing his place among the giants who have played this great game.

MARCEL DIONNE

Left: *Marcel Dionne labored in relative obscurity with the Los Angeles Kings before Wayne Gretzky made the Kings contenders. During his tenure in L.A. he quietly stacked up some remarkable numbers. Dionne is second only to Gordie Howe in 20-goal seasons, third in goals scored, and third in career points. When he resurfaced with the New York Rangers in 1988, it would be his final bow in the limelight.*

Every sport has had its share of underrated superstars, but the case of Marcel Dionne is special. Playing with quiet dignity throughout his 17-year career, Dionne flourished in relative obscurity in Los Angeles where hockey ranks somewhere between beach volleyball and star-gazing in popularity. Some would argue it was this pressureless atmosphere that allowed him to excel, but the facts show that Marcel Dionne ranks as one of the greatest to ever lace on the blades, regardless of where he skated.

Marcel Dionne had led the Ontario Hockey League in scoring for two straight years and was already touted as a superstar when he was drafted by the Detroit Red Wings in 1971. Although he didn't set the NHL on fire in his early years, he did show glimpses of the promise that was expected of him. What was not expected was his decision to leave Detroit and sign as a free agent with Los Angeles, the first hockey player to ever make such a bold move. If Marcel Dionne was afraid of the spotlight, he certainly didn't show it.

Dionne ignored the negative reaction to his controversial decision by answering his critics where it counted: on the ice. He became the offensive catalyst for the Kings, forcing a team of only mediocre talent to play to his level. His six 50-goal campaigns and seven journeys to the 100-point plateau that followed were capped off by capturing the Art Ross Trophy as the league's top scorer in 1980, when Dionne beat out a youngster named Wayne Gretzky to take home the silverware.

Dionne scored 20 or more goals in 17 consecutive seasons, second only to a man named Gordie Howe. In 12 of those winters, he fired home 30 or more goals, winning the Lady Byng Memorial Trophy in 1975 and 1977, and skating in eight All-Star classics. After a dozen campaigns in the City of Angels, Dionne was traded to the Big Apple where he took his act on one final tour on Broadway before hanging up the blades in 1988.

The list of Dionne's accomplishments is more than just impressive: third in goals with 731, third in points with 1,771, third in assists with 1,040 and twelfth in games played with 1,348. His name may not be on every fan's lips, but his name is on every page of the NHL record book. Statistics rarely tell the whole story, but they often tell the truth. In this case, the facts are simple: Marcel Dionne is one of the greatest superstars to ever pull on a jersey.

Right: *Dionne fends off a stick with a well-placed elbow. At 5' 8", Dionne was much smaller than many NHL players, but his size never kept Dionne from the center of action. He was a leader who forced teammates and opponents alike to play "heads up" hockey.*

Below: *Marcel Dionne:* "No one skates better and no one handles the stick better. He is a dynamic performer who may be the most exciting player to watch in the game . . . he just makes the puck dance." Bill Libby, The Hockey News, 1979.

MIKE BOSSY

Statistics rarely tell the whole story when discussing the qualifications of a superstar. Yet, in the case of Mike Bossy, the numbers he put in the record book during his 10-year career are so outstanding that they do give a true estimate of his value to the New York Islanders during his decade in the NHL. Mike Bossy scored 50 or more goals in each of his first nine seasons, becoming the first player to ever reach the 50 mark in tallies in his freshman campaign. He fired 60-plus goals on five occasions and reached the 100-point plateau seven times, establishing himself as one of the NHL's greatest right wingers. Add to this list three Lady Byng Memorial Trophies, the Calder Memorial Trophy and

Conn Smythe Trophy and you have the blueprint for stardom and the imprint of superstar.

The Islanders drafted Mike Bossy 15th in the 1977 amateur draft, which means 14 other teams had the opportunity to grab the Quebec Junior Hockey League graduate. It was an oversight each of those 14 teams would come to regret. The rap on Bossy was that his defensive game was below par, and while it was generally agreed that he possessed good shooting skills, many teams didn't rank him as an outstanding prospect. The Islanders ignored the negative reports on Bossy, concentrating on the potential of combining Bryan Trottier and Denis Potvin with this sharp-

shooter from Quebec. It was a move that would give the New York Islanders four return tickets into the Stanley Cup winner's circle.

It wasn't just that Bossy could score goals, it was how he scored them. As soon as the puck touched his stick, it was gone, usually headed for the top shelf or lower corner and past some beleaguered goaltender. Although he did not have great speed, Bossy became a craftsman at his position by perfecting the almost ancient art of the wrist shot. No winger in the NHL had a touch around the net like Mike Bossy, who employed his patented quick and deadly accurate release to lead the league in goals scored twice and

head up all post-season snipers on three occasions. On January 21, 1981, in a game against the Quebec Nordiques, Bossy climbed to a plateau many pundits thought to be unreachable. On that evening, the Montreal native scored his 50th goal of the season in his 50th game, becoming the first man since the immortal Maurice "Rocket" Richard to accomplish the feat.

A chronic back ailment that forced him to retire in 1988 may have written an early end to the Mike Bossy chapter in the NHL history book, but his name will always be on display in the NHL record book, and it is that distinction that places him here, as a superstar in the game of ice hockey.

DENIS POTVIN

Opposite top: *The Islanders' Captain Denis Potvin watches the shifting play and waits his time to spring into action.*

Opposite bottom: *Denis Potvin creates havoc in front of the Czechoslovakian goal during action in the 1976 Canada Cup final.*

Right: *A true franchise player, Potvin played his entire 14-year career with the New York Islanders, leading them to four straight Stanley Cup championships.*

From the moment that Denis Potvin pulled on a New York Islander jersey, it was clear that he was going to be a dominant force in the National Hockey League. The Islanders drafted the Ottawa native first overall in the 1973 amateur draft, and it's safe to say he exceeded all expectations. The rangy defenseman captured the Calder Memorial Trophy as the league's finest freshman in his first year in the bigs, but he was just starting to tap his vast potential. For the next 10 years, Denis Potvin was the offensive catalyst for the Islanders while controlling the tempo of the game from his rearguard position. Before Potvin arrived in New York, the Islanders had never won more than 19 games in a season. In his 14 campaigns patrolling the blueline in Long Island, the Islanders never finished below .500, never won fewer than 33 games, and never missed the post-season. When Potvin teamed up with Mike Bossy and Bryan Trottier, the Islanders were a force to be reckoned with.

During his years in the NHL, Potvin was continually compared to Bobby Orr, the great Boston defenseman whose style of play changed the game of hockey. Potvin adopted many of Orr's characteristics, but he brought his own special flair to the game. Blessed with outstanding mobility and a sniper's eye, Potvin led the Islanders out of the basement and into the penthouse. The Isles won four successive Stanley Cup championships with Potvin as their captain, taking home the silverware from 1979-80 to 1983-84. Potvin captured a host of individual awards as well, including eight All-Star berths and three James Norris Memorial Trophies as the league's best defenseman.

Potvin completely rewrote the NHL record book, setting new standards for defensemen in every aspect of the game. When he retired he was the career leader among defensemen in goals, assists and points. On April 4, 1988, in the second to last game of his career, he became the first NHL defenseman to register 1,000 career points. Potvin hung up the blades at the age of 34, not because he could no longer play the game, but because he could no longer play "his" game.

Although he always put team performance ahead of individual goals, the statistics tell us that Denis Potvin was one of the greatest to play his position, a true superstar in the game of hockey.

LANNY MCDONALD

One of the most beloved players to ever grace the arenas of the NHL, Lanny King McDonald played 16 seasons in the NHL with Toronto, Colorado and Calgary. Selected by the Maple Leafs in the first round (fourth overall) in the 1973 Amateur Draft, McDonald joined a Toronto team that was slowly rebuilding itself into a respected hockey franchise.

A renowned All-Star with the Medicine Hat Tigers of the Western Canadian Junior Hockey League, McDonald was teamed with Darryl Sittler and Errol Thompson when he arrived in Toronto, and the trio became one of the NHL's top offensive units. In 1977 McDonald scored 46 goals and collected 90 points to earn a berth on the NHL's Second All-Star Team. In the 1978 playoffs, he scored one of the most famous goals in recent Leafs history, a seventh game overtime marker that vaulted Toronto into the semifinals for the first time since 1967.

With his trademark mustache and skilled play, McDonald became an institution in Toronto. In 1979 he was caught in the middle of a power struggle between his best friend and teammate, Darryl Sittler, and the team's general manager, Punch Imlach. On December 29, 1979, an era came to a close in Toronto when McDonald was exiled to the Colorado Rockies, where he played for three seasons before being traded to the Calgary Flames.

In his first full season in Calgary, McDonald scored 66 goals, a total that earned him his second berth on the NHL's Second All-Star Team. At the post-season NHL awards banquet, McDonald went home with the Masterton Trophy and the King Clancy Trophy, two awards that recognized his work on and off the ice. Throughout his career, McDonald unselfishly donated his free time to the Special Olympics Program to provide athletic challenges for physically impaired children.

From 1983 to 1989, McDonald was the Flames' co-captain on the ice and a veteran voice in the dressing room. Throughout the 1980s, he made it his responsibility to keep his teammates focused on the ultimate goal, to win the Stanley Cup.

In 1988-89, McDonald reached the three milestones that he had set as career goals when he first entered the NHL in 1973-74. On March 7, 1989, in a game against the Winnipeg Jets, McDonald became the 23rd NHL player to reach the 1000 point plateau. Two weeks later, on March 23, the dandy Lanny slipped a shot past Mark Fitzpatrick of the New York Islanders for the 500th goal of his storied career.

In the 1989 playoffs, the Flames rolled through the post-season, defeating Vancouver, Los Angeles and Chicago to reach the Stanley Cup finals for the second time in franchise history. In a rematch against Montreal, the Flames entered game six in the Montreal Forum one win away from capturing the Stanley Cup. In the second period, with the score tied 1-1, McDonald took an ill-advised holding penalty. Seconds after leaving the penalty box, McDonald took a pass from Joe Nieuwendyk and fired a wrist shot past Patrick Roy to give the Flames a lead they would never surrender. It was his only goal of the playoffs and the last goal of his NHL career. In 1992 McDonald joined former teammate Darryl Sittler as an honored member of the Hockey Hall of Fame.

Left: *Lanny McDonald embraces the hallowed hardware after his game-winning goal against the Canadiens in the 1989 Stanley Cup finale. It was the last goal of McDonald's storied NHL career.*

Opposite: *Lanny McDonald began his Hall of Fame career in Toronto, where his trademark mustache and skilled play became an institution.*

GUY LAFLEUR

Opposite: *Guy Damien Lafleur combined his sharpshooting skills with a grace and presence on the ice that helped bring the Stanley Cup to Montreal five times.*

Right: *In his first three seasons in the NHL, Guy Lafleur showed little of the spark that made him the most-touted junior star of all time. In year four, he took off the helmet and his career took off as well.*

Overleaf: *Surrounded by New York Islanders, the toast of La Belle Province comes up with the puck in this 1990 tilt with his previous cross-town rivals, the Quebec Nordiques.*

If you were to invent the storybook hockey player, one who could skate like the wind, score at will, charm the entire hockey world, and lead one of the most successful teams of all time, you would invent Guy Damien Lafleur.

As the runaway star of the Quebec Major Junior Hockey League, Guy Lafleur was the most sought-after skater in the junior ranks. It was somehow fitting that he should have found himself the first choice overall in the 1971 amateur draft, and that the Montreal Canadiens were in a position to make that first pick. Like Jean Beliveau before him, the Forum faithful saw Lafleur as their own heritage property. When Beliveau hung up the blades following the 1970-71 season, his heir was waiting in the wings.

From the outset Guy Lafleur skated like he had always been in the big leagues. He played a decent, inconspicuous game for his first three seasons. Then, in 1974 he fired his first "more than 50" season, with 53 goals and 66 assists. This was a pattern that Lafleur would continue. The following year he became the Art Ross Trophy winner, as the biggest point-scorer in the league, a title he kept for three consecutive years. The Montreal Canadiens have paid the salary of some of the best sharpshooters in the history of the game, but never before had a member of the Habs' squad held the scoring title three years running.

Lafleur did not just score goals; he had a matchless grace on his skates, and the kind of presence known only to super-stars of every field. When "The Flower" entered a room, a rink, or a party, all eyes were drawn to him. He was the darling of la Belle Province, leading the Habs to six first-place finishes, five Stanley Cups, and into post-season play in every full season he skated.

By 1984 however, the Habs were no longer the NHL's most dominant team, and Lafleur was no longer the sniper he used to be. Though he could still skate like the wind itself, he had lost his scoring touch, and after suffering through an embarrassing drought, he decided to hang up the blades. In the summer of 1988, shortly before he was to take his place in the Hockey Hall of Fame, Lafleur announced he was coming out of retirement to play with the New York Rangers. Although many pundits thought he would never make it, the great Guy proved them wrong, playing with a new felt desire that has brought his fans back to the rink in droves. The Flower returned to Quebec to play with the Nordiques in 1989, and was the team's third-leading scorer, despite missing 41 games due to injury. Guy Lafleur retired after the 1990-91 season with no illusions or regrets. Though the "blond demon" no longer terrorizes enemy goaltenders, his spirit lives on in every NHL arena.

LARRY ROBINSON

Opposite: *A two-time winner of the James Norris Memorial Trophy as the league's best defenseman, Larry Robinson patrolled the Canadiens' blueline for 17 years, appearing in post-season play in each of those seasons.*

Right: *Larry Robinson made the move to sunnier climes in 1989, when he signed on with the Los Angeles Kings for the following season. Robinson's clean play and leadership have made him one of the most respected players on the circuit.*

In 1971 the Montreal Canadiens passed him over three times in the amateur draft. When their fourth pick came up, and 19 young men had been selected for big league teams, they gave the nod to Larry Robinson. Twenty years later, there were only two men from that draft still skating in the NHL. One of them, Guy Lafleur, is already is the Hall of Fame; the other, Larry Robinson, has a spot reserved for him in the honored Hall.

Robinson was a defenseman's defenseman. He didn't spend his time doing the forward's work; he stayed home, watched the shifting play, and awaited his time to make his move. He was a true puck lugger, whose job it always was to secure the disk, and bring it up to where his sharpshooters could put it to good use.

Some of the best defensemen have found intimidation and

brute force useful tools in their game, but not so with Larry Robinson. Though he would neither back down from a challenge, nor leave less physical players exposed to browbeating hulks, it was not Robinson's style to drop his gloves, or to waltz his opposition into the penalty box; Robinson averaged less than two minutes per game in the detention center.

Robinson played for the Montreal Canadiens for 17 years, recording post-season appearances in every one of these seasons, and won the Conn Smythe Trophy as the 1978 playoffs' Most Valuable Player.

A two-time James Norris Memorial Trophy winner, he was a smooth, fast skater and an on-ice quarterback of great renown. "Big Bird" Robinson retired in 1992 and is currently the assistant coach of the New Jersey Devils.

WAYNE GRETZKY

In 1990 Wayne Gretzky published his official autobiography. However, for many years the condensed version of his story has been updated annually; it's called the NHL record book. Not since Wilt Chamberlain arrived on the hardwood floors of the NBA has a player in any sport dominated the log of greatness as has Wayne Gretzky.

Gretzky has an uncanny ability that all athletes aspire to attain. He is not a great skater; he is by no means the best marksman, neither is he a big man, but he has managed to become the biggest star in the history of the game. The pundits say he is 20 seconds ahead of the play. He knows where the puck is at all times, and more importantly, he somehow seems to know where it's going. He doesn't pass the puck to his mates; he passes the puck to where his mates are headed, and his knack of timing in these situations is perhaps the key to his success.

Wayne Gretzky is used to being a superstar, it's a mantle he's worn since he was six years old. Since that time he has completely dominated every league in which he has played. Since he first laced up the skates, the media has focused on this skinny kid from Brantford, Ontario. Even the earliest film footage of him shows the loping style, the jersey tucked into his pants, and the patented victory salute of one arm and one leg thrust into the air. The media attention and the fantastic success has taught Gretzky how to handle pressure. He forgets about it and gets on with the game. We don't see Gretzky lose his cool, ever.

Since his days as a child prodigy, he has been compared to his idol, Gordie Howe. But as great as Gordie was, he never approached the kind of supremacy Gretzky has managed. Wayne Gretzky holds or shares over 59 National Hockey League records. The only offensive record he doesn't hold is career games played, and that is probably just a matter of time.

His 92 goals in 1981-82 may never be broken, and his 50 goals in 39 games that same year shattered what many felt was an indestructible record: Richard's 50 in 50. Four times he earned more assists than the next leading scorer had total points. In every international competition in which he has played, from World Junior Championships, to Canada Cups, to Challenge Cups, he has been the leading scorer. The Edmonton Oilers won the Stanley Cup four times while he was with the squad, and he led the playoff scoring on all occasions.

When he was traded in August of 1988, it was not only the biggest trade in hockey, or in sport, it was the biggest single news story of the year. It was also the biggest thing to happen to hockey in the United States since Lester Patrick. The trade of Wayne Gretzky to the Los Angeles Kings has not only revitalized hockey on the West Coast and paved the way to expansion in that part of the globe, it has made hockey a paying proposition in the United States.

In 1992-93, Gretzky led the Kings into the Stanley Cup finals for the first time. Although they lost to Montreal in five games, Gretzky led all playoff scorers with 40 points, the sixth time he has led the post-season scoring parade.

Opposite: *In 1982, when this photo was taken, the Edmonton Oilers' Wayne Gretzky was on his way to one of the most remarkable seasons in history. He scored 92 goals and 120 assists, shattering all previous records.*

Right: *Captain of the Los Angeles Kings, Wayne Gretzky continues to dominate the play of the NHL. The blockbuster trade which saw him go from Edmonton to Hollywood was the biggest Canadian news story of 1989.*

Overleaf: *The Great One looks for a breakout pass from his teammate. The energy and skill of sports' greatest superstar has raised the profile and the hopes of the Hollywood crew since Gretzky joined the Kings in 1989.*

RAYMOND BOURQUE

Bobby Orr was the main offensive instrument for the New England squad during the late 1960s and early 1970s great hockey revival in Boston. In the 1980s, the Bruins re-established themselves as a hockey powerhouse, and again a rearguard was the main catalyst behind the revitalized Beantown attack. This time the man's name is Bourque, and his dominance on the blueline in Boston brings back fond memories of his predecessors.

Ray Bourque was Boston's first round draft choice in 1979, and since that time, he has proven himself to be the NHL's steadiest rearguard. The Montreal native won the Calder Memorial Trophy in his freshman campaign and has been an All-Star in each of his 14 NHL seasons. His name has been engraved on the James Norris Memorial Trophy as the NHL's best defenseman four times and he has skated in every All-Star Game since he entered the League.

Blessed with break-out speed and almost unmeasurable dexterity, Bourque has redefined the role of the offensive defenseman. Like the man he is so often compared and contrasted with, Bourque has mastered Orr's uncanny technique of making a rush into the offensive zone and still returning to his defensive duties in time to prevent an opponent's scoring threat. This is all the more remarkable because, unlike the Boston teams of the 1970s, the Bruins' success in the 1980s depended upon defense.

It takes an outstanding athlete to combine these two disciplines, and it is a worthy testimony to the skills of Raymond Bourque that neither aspect of his game has suffered.

In his 14 campaigns patrolling the Beantown blueline, Bourque has averaged 21 goals and 78 points per season and he is the current team leader in almost every offensive category. For a rearguard, however, the name of the game is defense, and with Bourque cleaning up his own zone, the Bruins led the NHL in points in the 1980s and allowed the second fewest goals over the decade. Boston continued that dominance into the 1990s, leading the NHL in points in 1989-90 and making it into the Stanley Cup finals for the second time under Bourque's leadership. Boston may be the hub of the Eastern seaboard but Raymond Bourque is the center of attention in Boston Garden, a superstar who will skate into hockey immortality whenever he hangs up the blades on an outstanding NHL career.

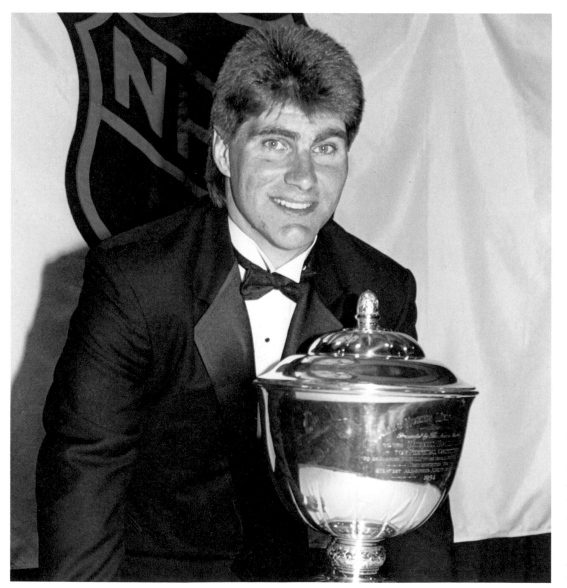

Left: *Bourque poses for the cameras in 1990, with his third Norris Trophy, the mark of the NHL's best defenseman. Like Bobby Orr before him, Bourque leads the Boston Bruins from behind the blueline, frequently figuring in the offensive game without shirking the defensive requirements of his position.*

Right: *The Stanley Cup crest on Bourque's chest and the determination in his eyes date this photo as a moment in the 1990 Stanley Cup final series. Bourque captained the Beantown Bruins into final play on two occasions, leading his team in the great tradition of the proud NHL franchise.*

Below: *Ray Bourque (#77) watches the shifting play, waiting for his moment to enter the fray in this 1990 confrontation with Wayne Gretzky's Los Angeles Kings.*

MARK MESSIER

The Hart Trophy has often been awarded to the NHL's leading scorer, sometimes neglecting the true meaning of the award. Officially it's an annual award to the player adjudged to be the most valuable to his team. Rarely has there been a more worthy recipient than Mark Messier, who captured the vaunted silverware in 1990 and 1992.

Mark Messier is simply the most competitive man on the NHL circuit today and in many pundits' eyes he is the league's most complete hockey player, combining scoring ability, perseverance, leadership and intensity. For many years he skated in the shadow of Wayne Gretzky, a role he never seemed to resent; for Messier, Wayne Gretzky meant having a winner in his corner, and that's the name of the game.

Like the Oilers of the early 1980s, Mark Messier was slow to mature, but by his third full season in the NHL he had begun to make his mark. He lit the red light 50 times during that campaign, but he considered the season a failure when the Oilers were swept out of the playoffs by the lowly Los Angeles Kings. After that point, the Oilers were a hockey dynasty, and Messier was their leader in the dressing room. After four Stanley Cups the Oilers faced the 1988 – 89 season without their on-ice leader, "Number 99." That season was a period of transition for the whole team, and Messier dropped below the 100-point mark for the first time

in three seasons. The 1989-90 campaign was a different story, however. Messier was handed the captain's jersey, and he took to his role with an intensity that kept the fans on the edge of their seats, and his teammates in awe. The Edmonton native carried his leadership duties onto the ice, registering a career year in every department; he racked up 129 points, to finish second in the NHL scoring race, a hair behind his former ice-boss, Wayne Gretzky.

Despite leading the Oilers to the Stanley Cup title in 1990, Messier was traded to the New York Rangers in 1991. The Rangers, who have been unable to win the Stanley Cup since 1940, needed an on-ice leader to provide skill and poise and an off-ice disciplinarian to motivate the troops. Messier proved to be the perfect fit. In his first season on Broadway, Messier transformed the Rangers into one of the NHL's finest teams. The 1990-91 Rangers set a team record with 50 victories and captured their first Presidents Trophy. In recognition for his achievements, Messier was awarded the Hart Trophy as league MVP, becoming only the second player to win the distinction with two different teams.

One of the strongest, most determined men in the National League today, Mark Messier has the respect of teammates, opponents, fans and critics, and is among the brightest lights in the hockey firmament.

Opposite: *You can trip him, hold him or hook him, but as this 1989-90 Stanley Cup final action photo indicates, you can't stop him. Bruin Bob Sweeney took a holding penalty for this ploy, but to slow down Mark Messier, you've got to do better than this.*

Right: *Traded to the Rangers in 1991, Messier helped the New Yorkers set a team record with 50 victories.*

Below: *Mark Messier is known as the best all-around player in the game today. When the Rangers won the Stanley Cup in 1994, Messier became the first player in NHL history to captain two different championship teams.*

PAUL COFFEY

Left: *A speedy defenseman with offensive aspirations, Coffey is able to control the flow of the game, and make the opposition play it his way.*

Opposite: *After seven productive years with the Edmonton Oilers, Coffey was the key man in a three-for-four trade which sent him to Pittsburgh. Having learned his trade by playing behind Wayne Gretzky, he understands the importance of feeding a prolific scorer, and teammate Mario Lemieux benefits tremendously from Coffey's early training.*

Like the black drink we start our days with, two things are true about Paul Coffey: He's not overly sweet, and he has the zip required to get the job done.

As one of the smoothest skaters coming out of the Ontario Hockey Association, Paul Coffey was just the man Glen Sather and the Edmonton Oilers needed to bring together one of the most winning units in the history of the game. Coffey was not known as a goal-scoring defenseman in his early days, but when he was teamed with likes of Wayne Gretzky, Mark Messier and Jari Kurri, Paul Coffey found scoring goals a natural part of his duties with the powerhouse Alberta squad. Coffey established himself as a superstar of the game when he fired 48 goals in 1985-86, the most by any blueliner in the history of the game. His 138 points that year is second only to Bobby Orr, the man who revolutionized the role of the defenseman.

Coffey had to learn his craft on the job, joining the NHL at the tender age of 19. He compiled only 32 points in that rookie campaign, and spent over two hours in the penalty box, but by the time he arrived at camp the next year, his skills and his body had matured. Over the next five years he averaged well over 35 goals per year, winning a fistful of honors.

He has been a seven-time All-Star, a three-time winner of the James Norris Memorial Trophy as the league's best defenseman, and a leader in the All-Star classic every year since 1982. Add to this his three Stanley Cup rings, and you

have the blueprint for a superstar.

Coffey spends a lot of time in the strike zone, but his speed allows him to do so without jeopardizing his defensive duties. Though he is a backliner, Coffey's abilities allow a team to count on him as a fourth forward player. Never one to back down from an opponent, Coffey can play the clutch-and-grab game as well as anyone, and when he skates off to the detention center, he usually takes an opponent along. One of the overlooked aspects of his game is his durability. He has played every game of the season in five separate campaigns, despite the beating to which a defenseman of his stripe is subjected.

Coffey has left a trail in the record books. He is the all-time career leader among defensemen in goals, assists and points, and in 1993-94 he became the first rearguard to compile 900 career assists. Yet, despite leading the Pittsburgh Penguins to the Stanley Cup in 1991, Coffey was traded to the Los Angeles Kings in 1992, joining his friend Wayne Gretzky. After only 60 games in the City of Angeles, Coffey was on the move again, this time to Detroit.

With his aggressive rushing style and his special team skills, Coffey has molded the Red Wings' powerplay into one of the NHL's foremost units. With Scott Bowman behind the bench and Sergei Fedorov and Steve Yzerman on the front lines, the Wings resemble the great Oiler teams of the 1980s. Of course, there's another similarity as well; the presence of Paul Coffey, NHL superstar.

AL MacINNIS

A perennial All-Star and one of the NHL's finest offensive defensemen, Al MacInnis has powered the Calgary Flames' attack for the past decade. With a wicked slap shot that is noteworthy for both its speed and its accuracy, this Nova Scotia native has become the mainstay of the Calgary Flames' defensive unit and a vital cog in what has become one of the NHL's most potent offensive attacks.

Although he was raised in the bitter winter climes of Canada's East Coast, MacInnis's hockey skills were fine-tuned in the hockey haven of Kitchener, Ontario, where he played for the Rangers, one of the Ontario Junior Hockey League's steadiest franchises. The Calgary Flames made him their Number 1 draft choice in 1981, and before he was even eligible to vote, he had already tasted the big league scene in Cowtown, having been brought up for a pair of tutorials in 1982 and 1983. After a short stay in the minors the following season, MacInnis was elevated to the top squad and from that moment "Big Al" has been a dominant force in the Calgary defensive strategy. Big, strong and mobile are the words most often used to describe this 6'2" giant, but the other labels most often pinned on him are mature, steady and overpowering. MacInnis has never scored fewer than 11 goals from his office on the blueline and

in his short stay in the bigs has developed one of the hardest shots to ever bend the hemp in the NHL.

MacInnis has surprised more than a few experts with his poise, especially in post-season play. He led all the spring-season performers in assists in 1986, when the Flames made their first appearance in the Cup finals. In 1988 he not only led all NHL snipers in playoff points, he also had his name placed alongside such immortals as Beliveau, Parent and Orr by winning both the Conn Smythe Trophy and the Stanley Cup.

In 1990-91, MacInnis became only the fourth defenseman to register 100 points in a single season, leading all NHL rearguards with 28 goals and 75 assists. A four-time NHL All-Star, MacInnis has represented the Flames in six mid-season All-Star Games and has reached the 20-goal plateau five times. One of the league's top blueliners, MacInnis continues to be the catalyst that ignites the Flames.

Below: *The 1989 playoff MVP Al MacInnis knows what it means to win the Stanley Cup.*

Opposite: *Looking to a brilliant future, this kid from Cape Breton Island has reached the pinnacle of success.*

MARIO LEMIEUX

The most high-touted prospect to enter the NHL during the 1980s, Mario Lemieux has matured into hockey's foremost talent. With a combination of instinct, skill and savvy, he has guided the Pittsburgh Penguins to a pair of Stanley Cup titles. But there is more to Lemieux than goals, awards and scoring records. No player has overcome greater adversity than the Magnificent Mario.

Pittsburgh drafted the Montreal native Number 1 in 1984, hoping that he would be the ticket to turn the franchise around. Although their playoff success has been limited to one appearance in the conference finals, the presence of number 66 has finally made hockey in Pittsburgh a viable business.

No one in today's game scores more exciting goals than Lemieux. Many times the highlights clips have shown him with defensemen all over him, dragging him to the ice, yet he still manages to get the shot off, and bank it in the net, to the frustration of his foes and the delight of his fans. As a measure of his greatness, one only needs to consult the NHL record book where his outstanding statistical achievements are well documented. He unseated Wayne Gretzky as the league scoring champion in 1988, engraving a new name on the Art Ross Trophy for the first time since 1981. The following year he became the first player since Phil

Above: *Mario Lemieux holds aloft the Stanley Cup after his Penguins defeated the Minnesota North Stars to win it all in 1991.*

Opposite top: *Lemieux in 1992 Stanley Cup action vs. the Black Hawks.*

Opposite bottom: *Lemieux has not missed an All-Star game in his career.*

Esposito in 1972-73 to lead the league in goals, assists and points, compiling 199 points, the third-highest single season total in NHL history.

One of only three players in league history to score 50 goals in less than 50 games, Lemieux led the Pittsburgh Penguins to back-to-back Stanley Cup championships in 1991 and 1992. Lemieux was the offensive catalyst in both Cup victories, leading all post-season scorers in '91 and '92 to become only the second player to win the Conn Smythe Trophy in consecutive seasons.

Already troubled with chronic back problems, Lemieux's health was threatened again in 1992-93, when he was diagnosed with Hodgkins Disease, a dangerous but treatable form of cancer. Yet, after only eight weeks of therapy, he was back on the ice, where he captured his fourth Art Ross Trophy as the league's scoring leader and solidified his position as one of the game's greatest players.

DOUG GILMOUR

When he was 13 years old, Doug Gilmour stood only 5′ 1″ and weighed less than 110 pounds. Still, he was a fiery competitor, determined to overcome the restrictions of his size. It wasn't going to be easy. After countless coaches told him he was too small to compete, Gilmour quit hockey. It was then that scout Gord Wood took him aside and encouraged him to continue playing. Wood put Gilmour on a Tier II team in Belleville, Ontario, where Coach Larry Mavety switched him from defense to forward. Wood later drafted Gilmour for the Ontario Hockey League's Cornwall Royals, and a future superstar was born.

Doug Gilmour's junior career with the OHL's Cornwall Royals was both memorable and productive. In his fresh-

man season, Gilmour compiled 119 points and helped the Royals capture their second consecutive Memorial Cup title with 15 post-season points. In his sophomore campaign of 1982-83, Gilmour was the OHL's best player, leading the league in assists (107) and points (177). Gilmour also established a league record by collecting at least one point in each of 55 consecutive games. That remarkable performance earned him the OHL's MVP Award and a seventh round draft selection by the St. Louis Blues.

Although he managed to reach the 20-goal plateau in each of his first three seasons in St. Louis, Doug Gilmour didn't hit his stride until the 1986 playoffs. Always noted for his ability to excel in pressure situations, Gilmour led the Blues to the Conference Finals, leading the team in shorthanded goals (2) and game-winning goals (2). Although the Blues were eliminated by the Calgary Flames, Gilmour tied for the playoff scoring lead with 21 points despite not making it to the finals. The following season, he had his finest campaign, scoring a career-high 42 goals and a team-leading 105 points.

In September 1988, Gilmour was traded to the Calgary Flames. In his first season in Alberta, Gilmour finished third in team scoring with 26 goals and 59 assists, while compiling a plus/minus mark of plus 45. In the post-season, Gilmour ignited the Flames, collecting 11 goals and 11 assists, while leading all Calgary skaters in shooting percentage (22.4) and plus/minus (plus 12). Gilmour's determination played a major role in Calgary's first Stanley Cup championship.

When he was dealt to Toronto in January 1991, many Maple Leaf fans were unaware of Doug Gilmour's skill and passion for hockey. However, it didn't take long for the success-starved Leaf fans to recognize Gilmour's impressive abilities. Almost immediately, the Leafs began to prosper, propelled by Gilmour's 49 points in 40 games. In 1992-93, the Leafs were one of the league's most improved franchises, with Gilmour as their undisputed offensive catalyst. He set career-high and franchise-high marks for points(127) and assists (95) in helping the Leafs achieve the finest season in the history of the franchise. Establishing himself as one of the NHL's dominant performers that season, Gilmour became the first Toronto player since Darryl Sittler to finish among the top ten scorers. In the post-season, he set another franchise mark with 35 playoff points, vaulting the Leafs to the Norris Division title. Although 1992-93 was his finest offensive season, Gilmour was also recognized for his tireless defensive play when he was awarded the Selke Trophy as the NHL's best defensive forward.

Opposite: *With his solid offense and tireless defensive play, Doug Gilmour won the Selke Trophy for his 1992-93 season, when his contributions helped the Leafs win the Norris Division title.*

Right: *Doug Gilmour in 1993 playoff action, when he set a Toronto Maple Leafs record with 35 playoff points. Since joining the Leafs in 1991, Gilmour has been the team's offensive catalyst.*

PATRICK ROY

The key to success for the Montreal Canadiens throughout their long history in the National Hockey League has been their ability to discover and tutor great goaltenders. From Vezina, to Durnan, Plante and Dryden, the last line of defense has always been among the most important characteristics of the Canadiens' team. When Patrick Roy arrived on the scene in 1985-86, fresh from the Quebec Junior Hockey League, he completed the puzzle that had kept the Habs out of the money since 1979.

With only 20 minutes of professional experience behind him, Roy took over the Number 1 goaltending job with the Habs, and had an impressive, though hardly outstanding, rookie campaign. When the Canadiens skated out for the playoffs that year, Roy's performance brought back memories of Ken Dryden's outstanding debut in 1971. Roy single-handedly led the Canadiens through the playoffs and into the Stanley Cup winner's circle, winning 15 games and compiling a microscopic goals against average of 1.92. He was rewarded for his efforts with the Conn Smythe Trophy as the league's MVP in the post-season. Since that time he has established himself as the NHL's greatest crease mogul, winning three Vezina Trophies, three Jennings

Above: *Patrick Roy in Game 1 of the 1993 Stanley Cup finals, helping Montreal win it all.*

Opposite: *Roy, who talks to his goal posts, epitomizes the notion that goalies are a different breed.*

Trophies (for fewest goals in the season) and five All-Star nominations.

The Vezina Trophy winner in 1991-92, Roy led the Montreal Canadiens to the Stanley Cup title again in 1993, leading all playoff goalies in wins (16) and goals against average (2.13). He also captured his second Conn Smythe Trophy, joining Bernie Parent, Bobby Orr, Wayne Gretzky and Mario Lemieux as the only repeat winners of the postseason MVP award.

Patrick Roy was an instant crowd favorite even among the most critical of hockey fans. His boyish looks, and his idiosyncrasies are now famous: he talks to his goal posts, cranes his neck like some weird giant bird, and approaches the game with a youthful whimsy which allows him to play this most arduous position with confidence.

Roy has won an individual award each year he has played in the NHL, assuring him a place among the stars.

BRETT HULL

Left: *Brett Hull, looking remarkably like his father, poses with the Lady Byng Trophy. Hull was named the most sportsmanlike player at the NHL awards for 1989-90.*

Opposite: *Said Bobby Hull of the Golden Brett: "Even at a very young age, if they got the puck to him in the slot, he could fire the thing. . . . He always had better action in his hands than many of the pro's I played with, right from day one."*

Brett Hull could have merely been Bobby Hull's hockey-playing son. With a father who ranks among the top players of any era, he was cursed and blessed with an almost impossible pair of skates to fill.

For Bobby Hull, greatness came naturally. He was a superstar in the NHL by the age of 18. For Brett Hull, things were considerably more difficult. Although he was blessed with his father's looks and his father's hard, accurate shot, he lacked the speed and burning desire of his patron. Despite racking up lofty numbers in United States college hockey, Brett Hull still needed a season of schooling in the American Hockey League before he was ready to "stick" in the NHL.

After a less than stellar start with the Calgary Flames, Hull was dealt to the St. Louis Blues, a team desperate for a sniper of his caliber. It was in St. Louis that he matured. Instead of spending his summers in leisure pursuits, the young Hull embarked on an intensive cross-training program, and when he appeared at camp to start the 1988-89 season, he was ready to take up the torch that his father had hoped to pass along.

In the 1988-89 season he lit the lamp 41 times and made his first appearance on the NHL All-Star roster. Pundits and players alike noted his new confidence and his new-found ability to handle the puck. Great things were once again ex-

pected of the Golden Brett, but nobody expected the explosion that was in store for the NHL's Norris division.

When Brett Hull arrived at 1989-90 training camp, his body had finally caught up with his ability. He had settled down and was ready to make his own distinctive mark in big league hockey.

The son of a superstar packs a lot of expectation into his equipment bag. His early years were burdened by constant comparison with his father, and Brett always ended up on the short side of the ledger. Now it was Brett Hull's turn on-ice: he would propel himself into the record books and out of the shadow that had dimmed his lights for years. In 1990 the Golden Brett arrived. He earned a spot on the NHL's first All-Star team, received the Lady Byng Memorial Trophy for most gentlemanly player, the Dodge Ram Tough Award for clutch performance, and led all NHL snipers with 72 goals, 14 more than his father had scored in his best NHL year.

In 1990-91, Hull became only the third player to score over 80 goals in a season, connecting 86 times to lead all NHL marksmen. A Hart Trophy winner and a three-time All-Star, Hull led the NHL again in 1991-92 with 70 goals, and added 54 more in 1992-93. With his sharpshooting and his style, the "Golden Brett" continues to be one of the NHL's most popular and successful superstars.

PAVEL BURE

From the first moment Pavel Bure stepped on the ice for the Vancouver Canucks at the Pacific Coliseum during the 1991-92 season, fans knew they were witnessing something special. A talented scorer who was as adept at playing right wing as he was patrolling the left side, Bure's offensive flair made him an instant star. In his third NHL game, he registered his first two goals, skating through the entire Los Angeles defense before slipping a pair of pucks past the Kings' Kelly Hrudey.

Nicknamed "The Russian Rocket" because of his explosive speed, Bure established a team record for goals by a rookie (34) while tying Ivan Hlinka's decade-old mark for freshman points (50). Bure added to his list of achievements by becoming the first Canuck to win the Calder Memorial Trophy as the NHL's best newcomer and the first Vancouver player to receive a major NHL award. Oddly, he also became the first Calder Memorial Trophy winner not to be

selected to the NHL's All-Rookie Team, not because he wasn't good enough, but because he was too good. Bure spent his rookie season playing both left and right wing, and when the year-end votes choosing the season's best rookies were tabulated, he had more votes than any other freshman, but they were split between both positions.

In his sophomore campaign of 1992-93, Bure became the first Vancouver Canuck to score 50 goals in a season, leading them with 60 goals and 100 points. He also became the first player since Phil Esposito in 1972 to register 400 shots on goal in a single season. The Rocket also tied for the NHL lead in shorthanded goals with seven, and was fifth in plus/minus with a plus 35.

Renowned as much for his defensive skills as for his offensive wizardry, Bure became the first Vancouver player to be voted by the fans to represent the Canucks at the NHL's annual All-Star Game.

Left: *In 1993 Pavel Bure became the first Vancouver Canuck to be voted by the fans into the NHL's All-Star Game. That season the Rocket led his team with 60 goals and 100 points.*

Above: *In his rookie season of 1991-92, Pavel Bure scored 34 goals on his way to winning the Calder Memorial Trophy as the league's best newcomer.*

Right: *A talented sharpshooter with speed and offensive flair, Bure tied for the league lead for shorthanded goals in 1992-93.*

JAROMIR JAGR

Although he has been in the NHL for only a few seasons, Jaromir Jagr has already established himself as an NHL superstar. A handsome young man with a ready smile, Jagr is a talented skater and a superb stickhandler with a flair for the dramatic. One of the league's most inventive players, Jagr is a magician with the puck, a rare commodity for a player of his large size. Many an NHL defenseman has been left red-faced after being duped by one of Jagr's patented "inside-out" maneuvers.

A first round draft selection of the Pittsburgh Penguins in the 1990 entry draft, he was the first Czech player to be able to attend the NHL entry draft without having to defect. Jagr spent two seasons with Kladno of the Czech National League, and in 1989-90 he led the team with 30 goals and 60 points in 51 games. He also played for the Czech Junior Team at the 1990 World Junior Championships, finishing second in tournament scoring with 18 points, and winning a spot on the round robin competition's All-Star Team. The following year, he made his NHL debut, collecting 27 goals and 30 assists to earn a berth on the NHL's All-Rookie Team. In the playoffs, he played a major role in the Penguins' drive to the Stanley Cup title, contributing 13 points to the cause in 24 post-season games.

Jagr's true value to the Penguins was illustrated in his second season. With Mario Lemieux on the shelf nursing a back injury, Jagr became one of the Penguins' offensive leaders, scoring 32 goals in 70 games. In the playoffs he was outstanding, compiling 24 points in 21 games. In game one of the Stanley Cup finals against Chicago, Jagr skated through the whole Chicago defense to tie the game with less than five minutes remaining. The Penguins went on to

Above: The Penguins' Jaromir Jagr breaks up a Black Hawk play in the fourth and final game of the 1992 Stanley Cup finals. Jagr's 24 points in 21 playoff games helped his team take the championship.

Opposite: Jagr showed his mettle in Game 1 of the 1992 Stanley Cup finals, when he skated through Chicago's defense to tie the game with less than five minutes remaining.

defeat the Black Hawks in four straight games, and many fans point to Jagr's goal as being one of the turning points in the series.

An established star when the 1992-93 season began, Jagr had the finest year of his career, collecting 94 points for the surging Penguins. Again, he was looked upon to provide leadership and opportunistic scoring when Mario Lemieux was forced out of the lineup with Hodgkins Disease. Jagr didn't disappoint his legion of fans, finishing third in the league with nine game-winning goals and fourth on the team with a plus/minus rating of plus 35.

A fan favorite around the NHL, Jagr has already been voted to the NHL's mid-season All-Star team three times, a remarkable achievement for a player who has only been playing in North America since 1990. A keen student of Czechoslovakian history, Jagr wears uniform number 68 as a tribute to the failed 1968 revolution. That sense of pride in his heritage, his personal aspiration to constantly upgrade his game and his effectiveness in the clutch have made Jaromir Jagr a respected NHL superstar.

FELIX POTVIN

The goaltender is the backbone of every successful team. In the 1970s and early 1980s, Montreal, Boston, Philadelphia and the New York Islanders won 14 Stanley Cups between them, often on the merits of great goaltending. The men who led those teams to the championship – Ken Dryden, Bernie Parent, Gerry Cheevers and Billy Smith – are all members of the Hockey Hall of Fame, a worthy reward for their outstanding play. The Toronto Maple Leafs and their fans believe that Felix Potvin has the ability and the mental toughness necessary to bring the Stanley Cup back to Ontario. It's no coincidence that the rebirth of the Toronto franchise has coincided with the arrival of Felix Potvin in the National Hockey League.

A two-time All-Star with Chicoutimi of the Quebec Major Junior Hockey League, Potvin led the loop in shutouts in each of his three seasons in the league. In 1991 he led Chicoutimi to the Memorial Cup finals, where he was selected as the outstanding goaltender of the round robin tournament. A member of the gold medal-winning Canadian National Junior Team at the 1991 World Junior Hockey Championships, Potvin was also named the Canadian Major Junior Goaltender of the Year for the 1990-91 season.

Selected by Toronto in the second round of the 1990 entry draft, Potvin made his NHL debut during the 1991-92 season, replacing the injured Grant Fuhr in the Leafs' nets. Although he failed to record a victory in his four-game stint

Opposite: *Drafted by Toronto in 1990, Felix Potvin earned the starting goaltender's job in 1992-93, compiling a league-low goals against average mark of 2.50.*

Right: *Potvin's unique goaltending style is a key to his success. In 1993-94 he became the first Leaf player selected by the fans to represent his team at the All-Star classic.*

Below: *With a quiet confidence that belies his lightning-fast reflexes, Potvin has become a fan favorite and an NHL superstar.*

in the NHL, Potvin was spectacular, allowing only eight goals for a goals against average of 2.39. Potvin spent the majority of the 1991-92 campaign with the St. John's Maple Leafs, winning the American Hockey League Rookie of the Year Award as well as capturing the Baz Bastien Trophy as the league's top goaltender.

One of the keys to Potvin's success is his unique goaltending style. He remains deep in his net, relying on his rapier-fast glove hand to snare rising shots. In scrambles in front of the net, he crouches low and lays his stick along the ice to block low shots, while keeping his shoulders square to the shooter. He also utilizes his blocker in an inventive way, deflecting shots into the corners so they can be easily cleared by his defensemen.

In 1992-93, Potvin's outstanding play earned him the Number 1 goaltender's job, allowing the Leafs to trade Grant Fuhr to Buffalo. If the pressure bothered the young rookie, he didn't show it. He became the first Leaf rookie to lead the NHL in goals against average since Al Rollins in 1951, compiling a league-low mark of 2.50. In the playoffs, he led the Leafs to the semifinals for the first time since 1978 before losing a heartbreaking seven-game series to the Los Angeles Kings.

Potvin's quiet confidence and grace under fire has made him a fan favorite throughout the NHL. In 1993-94, he became the first Leaf player to be selected by the fans to represent his team at the NHL's annual All-Star classic. A winner wherever he has played, Felix Potvin has earned the honor of being called an NHL superstar.

ERIC LINDROS

During the 1980s, the NHL was dominated by two players: Wayne Gretzky and Mario Lemieux. Throughout the hockey community, scouts and general managers were on the outlook for the "Next One," the player with the potential to control the game of hockey in the 1990s.

At this time, Eric Lindros was playing for the prestigious St. Michael's College in midtown Toronto. One of the richest breeding grounds of pedigree hockey talent in the history of the game, St. Mike's has sent such future Hockey Hall of Famers as Frank Mahovlich, Tim Horton, Red Kelly and Dave Keon into the NHL. The school also maintains high academic standards, which was equally important to the Lindros family. Lindros stood out among his peers, and not only because he was a 6′ 2″, 220-pound teenager. Lindros was a whirling dervish on the ice, as adept at crashing opponents into the boards as he was at maneuvering

through the defense before slipping the puck past a confused goaltender.

Unique in another way, Lindros believes that an athlete should be able to choose where he would ply his trade. When the Sioux St. Mary Greyhounds of the Ontario Hockey League made him their first selection in the midget draft in 1989, Lindros refused to play for the Northern Ontario team. Instead, he joined the Detroit Compuware of U.S. Hockey League, where he collected 52 points in only 14 games. In January 1990, the Greyhounds traded Lindros to the Oshawa Generals, a team near Toronto where the great Bobby Orr had played junior. In his first full season in Oshawa, Lindros led the OHL with 149 points and guided the Generals to the Memorial Cup championship.

As the top-ranked junior in North America, it was clear that Lindros would be the first selection in the 1991 NHL

Left: *Despite missing part of his 1992-93 freshman campaign due to injury, Eric Lindros set a Philadelphia rookie record with 41 goals. The Quebec Nordiques traded Lindros to the Flyers after he refused to play for them.*

Opposite top: *In 1991 Eric Lindros became the first non-professional to play for Team Canada in the Canada Cup Tournament. He was also part of the 1992 medal-winning Canadian Olympic Team.*

Opposite bottom: *Eric Lindros combines power and agility on the ice.*

entry draft. The trump card in that draft deck was held by the Quebec Nordiques, who finished last in the NHL standings in 1990-91. Although Lindros made it clear to the Nordiques' officials that he was not interested in playing in the "small market" atmosphere of Quebec City, the Nordiques still made him the first pick of the 1991 rookie auction. True to his word, Lindros declined to report, insisting he was prepared to return to junior rather than play in Quebec.

As the Nordique stalemate continued through the 1991-92 season, Lindros joined Team Canada for the 1991 Canada Cup Tournament, becoming the first non-professional to play for the squad. He later skated for the Canadian Olympic Team at the 1992 Winter Olympics, helping the Canadian team win its first medal since 1968.

In June 1992, the Quebec Nordiques finally traded Lindros, sending the talented centerman to the Philadelphia Flyers for six players, two first round draft choices and millions of dollars in cash. Despite missing 23 games of his freshman NHL campaign with a knee injury, Lindros set a Philadelphia rookie record with 41 goals. More importantly, he has revived the fortunes of the Philadelphia franchise, and stands poised to lead the Flyers through the 1990s and back into the Stanley Cup winner's circle.

TEEMU SELANNE

Left: *Teemu Selanne played for his native Finland in the 1991 Canada Cup Tournament. In 1992 the "Finnish Flash" took his act to the NHL's Winnipeg Jets.*

Opposite: *Athletic and intuitive, Selanne led NHL rookies in goals, points, powerplay goals and game-winning goals in his 1992-93 freshman season.*

No rookie who ever laced on his skates in the NHL made a greater impact on the league than the "Finnish Flash," Teemu Selanne. Touted as one of the finest European-trained prospects to ever cross the ocean and play in North America, Selanne set new standards for NHL freshmen in his first professional campaign of 1992-93. The first Finnish player to be selected in the first round of the NHL entry draft, Selanne established NHL rookie records for goals (76) and points (132). In addition to winning the Calder Memorial Trophy and earning a berth on the NHL's First All-Star Team, the Helsinki native became the first rookie since Roy Conacher in 1939 to lead the league in goals.

The Winnipeg Jets, an organization that focuses on finding top-notch European talent, had made Selanne their first choice in the 1988 entry draft. One of the top scorers in the Finnish National League, Selanne had decided to stay in Europe with his Jokerit team instead of moving into the professional ranks in North America. This gave the skilled right winger the opportunity to play for his country at the 1991 Canada Cup tournament and in the 1992 Winter Olympic Games. After leading the Finnish league with 39 goals in 44 games in 1991-92, Selanne decided the time was right to move his game to the next level, the NHL.

One of the factors delaying Selanne's move to the NHL was a lingering contract dispute with the Winnipeg Jets. Because Selanne had been unable to come to terms with the

Jets, he became a restricted free agent, which meant any team could make him a contract offer, but if the Jets matched the terms, Selanne would have to sign with Winnipeg. In the summer of 1992, the Calgary Flames offered Selanne a multi-year, multi-million dollar contract. Although the Jets play in a small market community with tight financial limitations, they matched the deal, making Selanne one of the richest rookies in NHL history.

Selanne wasted no time in rewarding his new employers for their investment. He collected his first NHL point in the Jets' opening game, and scored his first NHL goal two days later. He was an instant hit with the fans, generously giving his time to community and charitable causes while being cast as the first superstar to suit up for the Jets since the departure of Dale Hawerchuk. On the ice, he was a blossoming superstar, leading all NHL rookies in goals, points, powerplay goals and game-winning goals. He set a Jets record with at least one goal in eight consecutive games, and became the first Winnipeg player to record a post-season hat trick, firing home three goals against the Vancouver Canucks in the Smythe Division semifinals.

Blessed with soft hands and above average speed, Selanne has the unteachable ability to always be one step ahead of the play. Relying as much on instinct as he does on athletic ability, Selanne's natural goal-scoring skills insure that he will be a hockey superstar throughout the 1990s.

INDEX